MARRIAGE

How To Keep A Good Thing Growing

MARRIAGE

How To Keep A Good Thing Growing

JOHN W. DRAKEFORD

ZONDERVAN PUBLISHING HOUSE
OF THE ZONDERVAN CORPORATION
GRAND RAPIDS, MICHIGAN 49506

Library of Congress Cataloging in Publication Data

Drakeford, John W.
  Marriage, how to keep a good thing growing.

  Reprint. Originally published: Nashville, Tenn. : Impact Books, c1979.
  1. Marriage.   I. Title.
HQ734.D82   1982   646.7'8   82-20020
ISBN 0-310-70081-7

Printed in the United States of America

83 84 85 86 87 / 10 9 8 7 6 5 4 3

Dedicated To:
Howard and Mary D. Walsh,
two actionists
whose amazing variety of activities
are a wonder to their friends.

TABLE OF CONTENTS

Introduction

In a recent magazine article the family is reported to be "down but not out." With that, many a reader heaved a sigh of relief. At last, some good news—not the best, but more hopeful than some statistics would lead us to believe.

Marriage, the basic ingredient of family life, has certainly taken a pasting over the last few years and the prophets of gloom have had a heyday predicting its demise. But don't count the family out too soon! Even some of those who elected to bypass this discredited institution are apparently having second thoughts. Some women who decided to sidestep the walk to the altar and just "live" with a man have now taken legal action to get the share of his assets to which a legally married wife would be entitled. One of the really strange aspects of all this is the statement by a television personality that in consideration of such cases, "We may have to reinvent marriage!"

The propaganda that has been permeating our society is

the not-so-subtle message that marriage as an institution has failed. When a prominent journalist announced her intention to marry, she was met with the response, "Oh, that's too bad." The implication was, "Why is a nice girl like you getting married?" Picking up a magazine, the journalist ran across an ad for a popular psychological publication. The ad portrayed a smiling mother, father, and three happy children. The arresting caption read: "This family will self-destruct in five years or sooner. This man and this woman will find it impossible to live with each other under the pressures and pretense that marriage, family, and society will place upon them."

Such advertising with its strong anti-marriage sentiment easily becomes a self-fulfilling prophecy. The idea has been reinforced in the mind of the modern reader because it comes from a psychology publication—psychology being the new deity worshipped by a large proportion of our population.

This anti-marriage propaganda has pervaded our society in many and varied forms:

- Two children are playing. Girl: "Let's play house." Boy: "I'd rather play divorce. You get the house and I get the car."

- Entertainer: "We used to think marriage was a contract, but Hollywood is trying to convince us it is only a ninety-day option."

- Woman on plane to fellow passenger after learning he is a marriage counselor: "I sure could use your services. I'm on my eighth divorce."

- Lecturer: "Americans believe in serial polygamy. They have a number of wives but not all at the same time."

- Las Vegas wedding chapel marquee: "Weddings conducted here—everything provided. Divorces—next door."

The movement to downgrade marriage and family has developed a certain momentum and created a climate that may be represented by the statement, "The family is out of favor." Much of this has come not so much because of the failure of an institution as the failure of people. Having failed in marriage, it is a simple step to adopt a sour grapes attitude that points an accusing finger at the institution rather than the participants.

Marriage is a growth experience, but we Americans are not particularly keen on the growing process. Ours is a youth culture. Just look at the attention lavished on our children and young people. Small wonder no one wants to grow up. The result is a generation of adult-size children. If you will examine medieval paintings, you'll discover the children appear as miniature adults. Gaze on the tableaus of life today and you'll see adults who look like wrinkled adolescents. The fragility of many modern marriages may be mute testimony to the immaturity of its partners. Nothing much has changed since Jesus likened the generation of his day to "children playing in the market place."

Like the pathetic child brides of India, nursing babies when they should be holding dolls, we have many husbands and wives who are ill-prepared for marriage. It is much easier, for example, to get a license to marry and to bring children into the world than it is to get a license to drive an automobile. The reasoning behind licensing drivers for the highway is that drivers who cannot pass a driving test and have insufficient knowledge of highway laws might hurt somebody. Consider the awful potentialities for damage that lie in an ill-conceived marriage with children unthinkingly brought into the world only to be cast loose as a charge on the community.

Mature people make mature marriages. The viability of a marriage may be an indication of the stability of the marriage partners. Successful marriages are frequently overlooked in our warped society. The scenario of a successful executive includes the faithful wife who stands beside him through thick and thin as he struggles to get the key to the executive restroom. Once he has attained to the new corporate status, he sees a more attractive, generally younger woman, and casts aside his faithful partner of the years. The new, youthful, and more sophisticated wife may become as much a symbol of his new status as the chauffeured limousine that whisks him to his seat of power.

It may not be that way in actual reality. A recent study of the top executives in the U.S. showed that the stereotype of the successful executive shedding wives might be far from the truth. The Grant Study followed the fortunes of 268 Yale students. Most of these men went on to become eminently successful in their field. Later, a psychiatrist randomly selected ninety-five of the men for testing. Of these, nineteen were company presidents and the research concluded they had the most enduring marriages and solid relationships with their children.

The results of this study intrigued the editors of *Town and Country Magazine* who researched the family life of presidents of the top 100 companies in the U.S.A. and discovered only five percent of them had ever been divorced. Compared with the national average of thirty-five percent of first-marriage failure, it seems that unusual capacity in the business world may be an indication of ability to relate to others. One comment on the findings is that the indications are that the capable business president is "mentally healthy" and his mental health may be indicated by his ability to maintain good marriage and family relations.[1]

The media, depending as it does on sensationalism to capture the reader's attention, pays little attention to statistics like these and is seldom attracted by routine marriage and family relationships. The constant note of the media has been news of the multiplication of divorces and dissolution of the family. They overlook the significant fact that 60 percent of all husbands and wives stick together until death brings the parting. With the increased longevity of human beings, it follows that the marriages that last do so for many more years than ever before.

A new day is dawning in the field of medicine. In the past, medical doctors have spent the greatest proportion of their time helping sick people to get well. Now a movement emphasizing preventative medicine is cautiously emerging. The dedicated doctors in this field have a low profile. Not for them the drama of the operating room, green-gowned surgeons, pretty nurses, blips sailing across screens, the news conference to reveal the dramatic way in which the patient was snatched from the jaws of death. Rather, theirs is the careful assessment of the condition of the patient, suggestions as to appropriate action to forestall possible illnesses, steps to take to strengthen a weakened organ. This type of medicine has had to fight for recognition. Faced with the skyrocketing costs of hospital care and doctors' fees, it seems there would be a stampede toward preventative medicine. There is some evidence of a move in this direction with such measures as annual checkups, exercise programs, and strategies to improve general health, but the movement is slow.

So it is in the field of family relations. The difficulties, dramatic confrontation, and lurid details of affairs have widespread interest. Like so many in the field I started with counseling, trying to put broken lives back together. I soon learned that if the husband and wife were already in court in the process of seeking a divorce and the judge had ordered counseling, the prognosis for success was poor. Usually, by this time, the relationship had deteriorated too far. On the other hand, if the marriage were not in a serious state of disrepair, there were good prospects that something could be accomplished.

The thought occurred: Why not get to these people *before* the catastrophe! *Instead of an ambulance at the foot of the cliff, why not build a railing at the top to prevent them from falling over in the first place?*

From this concept has come the commitment to help strengthen family life. In the beginning of our family conferences, some people were reluctant to attend. Their excuse: "If we go to that conference people will think we are having trouble." So the nomenclature was changed and we referred to our efforts as *Family Enrichment Conferences.* One publicity piece depicted a silver vase with the statement, "No matter how fine the silver, it can always be polished." No marriage is so bad that it cannot be helped and none so good that it cannot be improved.

This book is a marriage maintenance manual. It is preventative medicine for marriages. Here are fourteen basic strategies aimed at strengthening marriage. They are *action* strategies—things you can do individually and as a couple to enrich your marriage. The aim of this book is to make your marriage into a relationship ready for any contingency—a marriage for all seasons.

Action Strategy #1

DO SOMETHING—THE DECISIVE MOTIVATIONAL ACTION

"The happiness of pursuit"

"Do you, John Thomas, take this woman, Mary Harris, to be your lawfully wedded wife?"

"I do."

"And do you, Mary Harris, take this man, John Thomas, to be your lawfully wedded husband?"

"I do."

The words "I do" are so indelibly associated with marriage that a popular musical on the frailties of the wedded life is called "I Do! I Do!" In the true spirit of many marriages, the appropriate title would be "I Don't! I Don't!" or perhaps "I Won't! I Won't!"

Marriage is many things. It is an event, a ceremony that takes place at a given moment of time: "I was married on the seventh of June." It is an experience: "They were married and lived together happily for many years." It is a condition: "He is a married man." The event and the experience take place in a point in time. The condition of marriage can just as easily be thought of as a static situation. However, the basic hypothesis of this book is that MARRIAGE IS NOT A CONDITION. IT IS A WAY OF LIFE—AN ACTIVITY.

Swiss philosopher Rougemont used to say marriage killed romance. In arguing his case, he claimed romance was a perpetual chase. The beloved object was like some will-o'-the-wisp, deftly slipping away from the eager suitor's outstretched hands. Marriage, on the other hand, brought certainty which ended the pursuit and so romance died. There may be another way of looking at Rougemont's idea. The flavor of the relationship in romance might not have been so much the *uncertainty* as the *action*. The aspiring lover was *doing something* and in the process enjoyed the sense of exhilaration.

Ask any knowledgeable person about the difference between an American and an Englishman and there is a good chance he will say the Englishman is more conservative, more staid, more stiff-upper-lip while the American is more energetic, brash, and a hustler. If you apply that criterion to riders of the escalator you are wrong, wrong, wrong.

Mount an escalator in an American airport, and you'll find people largely ignoring signs that suggest, "Standers to the right, walkers to the left." The riders drape themselves in various poses across the moving palisade and stand chatting with friends or gazing out into space—looking as if they are taking a leisurely cruise down the river on a Sunday afternoon.

Contrast this scene with that in a British subway. The tired commuters who don't feel like walking stand close to the side, leaving a clear run for those who are in a hurry. This happy breed of hustlers goes hurrying on up or down the stairways, and if an American gets in the way, may politely protest, "I say, old chap, would you mind moving over?"

Move on or move over—that's the message of life and it is just as certainly the message of marriage.

Just because you want to dawdle along does not mean

that no one else needs to get by. They are going to move on and you're going to be left behind. *Even though you're on the right track, you're going to be run over if you stand still.*

While your marriage is languishing and you are feeling satisfied to let it remain that way, there are other people who are going to take advantage of your situation.

From Attitude to Action

For many years now, motivational books have been majoring on people's "attitudes." So has come the highly successful P.M.A.—"Positive Mental Attitude." The trouble with attitudes is they can be static.

The word *attitude* comes from the word *aptitude* and literally means "posture." It was used originally for describing the Greek athlete in a posture of readiness—readiness to respond to the starting signal. But what if the athlete were forever frozen in this position and never sprang into action? Always on the starting line, but never took off down the track?

The Positive Mental Attitude must move to another level—the action level. P.M.A. now becomes D.M.A.—the "Decisive Motivational Action."

The plan set forth here is that action—not just any action—but action of a certain type—the *decisive motivational action* may be the secret of a new era in married life! While each word in this statement is of primary importance, it is basically and preeminently a plan of action.

In recent years a whole new breed of people has come to the fore. They are the activists—those who are disturbed by some aspect of society and are determined to change things. They are not satisfied to wait for an evolutionary development of society but insist something must be done immediately. Because they are sometimes vociferous in their condemnation of the prevailing system and may go so far as to advocate its destruction, the term activist has developed some unfortunate connotations.

The ideal set out here will be of the *actionist* rather than the activist. We will focus on the action of husbands and wives in a significant unit of society that is generally referred to as the family. They are not out to change others, but to improve themselves and their marriage relationship. They may ultimately start something that could change a number of other people or even a wider segment of society, but that is not their primary task, nor that of this book.

We may face another dilemma for it is so easy for us to major on the lack of action—what we do not do. I went into the army happily and proudly. World War II days in the part of the world where I lived were devoid of protestors, and a warm patriotism coupled with an awareness of significant national threat propelled me into uniform. As a chaplain I was conscious of my spiritual responsibilities and determined to stand by, what some might call, my somewhat puritanical convictions.

My first test came when the colonel met me at the club and introduced me to my fellow officers. "How about a whiskey?" he asked jovially. I swallowed, "Thank you, sir, but I don't drink." As we stood chatting, a major offered me a cigarette. "I appreciate it, but I don't smoke." About this time a bright-eyed lieutenant came rushing up, "Hi. Say you're new here, aren't you? We are having a dance on Saturday night and need another man to escort one of the nurses. How about it?" I gulped again, "Sorry, I don't dance."

A suntanned captain had been observing all of this and at last he spoke, "Chaplain, do you spit?"

All my virtues were negatives.

Not too much unlike some husbands and wives—right? As they sit discussing their marriage with a counselor, many a husband or wife take great delight in parading their negative virtues:

"I don't drink."

"I don't smoke."

"I don't gamble."

"I don't stay out at night."

"I never run around on her."

"I've never refused him."

"I've not neglected the children."

Some theologians speak about two types of sins, sins of commission, the things we have done which we shouldn't have done, and sins of omission, things we have left undone which we ought to have done. In our discussion we will concentrate on sins of omission—actions we should have taken.

Might-Have-Been Marriage

Few people take a hostile approach to the family. Most of us realize the importance of this basic unit of society and really want to succeed in our marriage relationship. But goodwill and good intention are not enough. "Happily ever after" may be only a myth if we enter marriage believing it is automatically going to be a transforming experience.

Napoleon Bonaparte used to say that every French soldier had a marshall's baton in his knapsack. I am equally convinced that a good proportion of the literate population have a book in their heads. Whenever I'm introduced to people as an author, there is always at least one and generally more than one person who says, "You're an author? I'm going to write a book."

I respond, "I'd like to read it."

"Oh, I haven't written it yet, but," tapping his head,

"I've got it in here. I'm going to write it down someday—when I have time."

I murmur something about wishing the would-be writer well: "I hope your book is a best-seller."

If I were honest I'd say, "Millions of people have thought about writing a book. But you don't have a book until you act—put it down on paper."

The Positive Mental Attitude must move on to another stage—there must be some action.

Few poems about man/woman relationships are more moving than Whittier's "Maud Muller," which tells of a country maiden and a judge who have a brief encounter in which he asks for, and she gives him, a drink of water. In the following years they go their separate ways. Both are dissatisfied with their marriage and each often dreams of the other and the way marriage "might have been" for them. The poet concludes his versifying:

> Alas for maiden alas for judge
> For rich repiner and household drudge
> . . . .
> Of all the sad words of tongue or pen,
> The saddest of these: It might have been.

What happened? The wedding was planned to the last detail. No expense had been spared. Everything seemed set for an idyllic marriage that had everything going for it. Then the sky fell in. Apparently there are things that cannot be bought with money. Dreams alone are never enough. There must be action. If there is no action, the principals may later mourn, "It might have been."

Generating the Power

Emerson used to say, "Do the thing and you shall have

the power; but they who do not the thing have not the power." There is a cycle whereby motivation creates an action which in turn builds stronger motivation.

It is imperative that marriage actions have a strong *motivational* objective. Mere practice without any thought may accomplish little or nothing. The word *motivate* relates to the goad, the spur that drives an individual. This is a motivational program—one that will prod you on from one level to another. When we move on from attitudes, we don't mean to discard the attitude supposition but rather to take attitudes on to a new action level.

I am thinking of my childhood days when we managed through the winter with the scant warmth coming from a simple wood fire. When we retired in the evening we kept warm by piling on the blankets and covers and putting our feet on bricks, warmed and wrapped in newspaper. Body warmth fended off the cold of the winter's night, but rising in the morning was a real test of character. We knew nothing of the luxury of carpets. Our bedroom floor was covered with linoleum kept shining bright with frequent applications of polish by my industrious mother. Unfortunately, linoleum has an affinity for coolness and this was a major hurdle for the early riser. That shining floor looked like the surface of an ice skating rink. Lying there in the warm bed with just the top of my head visible, I would summon all my strength, throw aside the bedclothes, and race across the floor.

That move launched me abruptly into a new day. The action a husband and wife take individually or jointly in connection with the plan of this book is an adventure in faith that will lead into some new experiences and pathways in married life. As we proceed through the book, we will come to understand that action is a learning process—we learn by doing. The result of the action will change some things within yourself and your marriage.

The Decisive Move

The D.M.A. advocated herein represents a crisis point—a definite commitment—a deliberate involvement. The action must be decisive—not something done languidly or casually. You can't do it by inches.

Mrs. Marsh, the head nurse of a hospital floor, taught me this valuable lesson. This lady knew how to handle men as I found to my initial dismay and later delight. I had the misfortune to break my leg. When I was admitted to the hospital, the enthusiastic but inexperienced young intern decided to cover my injured limb from the top of my thigh to the sole of my foot with strips of adhesive tape. The job completed, my leg looked as if it had been borrowed from an Egyptian mummy at the museum.

Then came the verdict from the orthopedic surgeon that the situation called for surgery. The tape must come off. An orderly apologetically started on the job. I writhed in agony and protested every inch of the tape he gingerly tried to pull off. The head nurse, Mrs. Marsh, happened by, saw my predicament, and acted decisively. "Look toward the wall," she instructed. Then taking hold of the end of the tape, she gave it a mighty yank. Wow!! It was off. So it proceeded, punctuated with my fierce protests and her equally adamant commands to "Look at the wall." Afterward, I lay there contemplating my hairless, reddened, tenderized leg and realized what might have been a couple of hours of misery was over and done within five minutes.

Mrs. Marsh was every inch a professional from her smart, deft movements to her calm, definite manner. She was capable of making decisive moves that under more serious circumstances could save lives.

The actions you will learn in this book are decisive,

sometimes painful, but they must be taken. You are going to have to get with it. When you act you will suddenly discover an unexpected increment. The decisive movement brings with it a certain lift of the spirit, a joy that comes from acting—doing something.

The Faith Element

An indispensable part of this program is the faith element. Christian faith implies an action program. Faith and action go hand in hand and, while action may play some part even in generating faith, faith most certainly is a strong motivation toward action. So much so that James says, "Faith without works is dead" (2:26, KJV). Faith is the motivating force within human personality that leads to action.

Jesus spoke about a faith that could remove mountains and in the strangest ways this projection has become reality. Some men stood before a mountain in Tasmania, an island south of continential Australia. As they surveyed it, a strange materialistic faith crept into their hearts. A lode of copper waited there within the mountain to be unearthed. Workers were brought in and machines installed. Great pumps set to work and began to literally wash away the mountain in search of the valuable metal buried beneath the surface. Faith resulting in action literally moved a mountain. There are more significant mountains than those to be moved in the marriage relationship.

Study the eleventh chapter of the epistle to the Hebrews frequently called the "Faith Chapter." The chapter opens with a magnificent statement of faith: "Faith is the substance of things hoped for, the evidence of things not seen" (11:1, KJV). The rest of the chapter describes the great heroes of faith. We know of their faith by their actions.

Jesus, the gentlest of all people, seldom lost his temper but when he did express himself, it was in no uncertain terms. His condemnation of one man was that he should be cast into outer darkness, a horrible place where there would be weeping and gnashing of teeth (Matt. 22:13 KJV).

What was this man's sin? Adultery? Murder? Hypocrisy? Lying? Stealing?

No, none of these. He did nothing—absolutely nothing—and because he did nothing, he was condemned to an awful fate.

The Savior is on the side of the actionist.

The Decisive Motivational Action

Action is the focal point of this volume—not just any action but action which moves through at least three well-defined phases, each of which is built on a basic principle.

• **THE ACTION PRINCIPLE.** *We begin our quest by considering action per se. Our first basic concept is that movement is life—move and live.*

• **THE MOTIVATIONAL PREMISE.** *While movement is an indication that life exists, an unconscious person kept physically alive by support systems may have certain movement within his body but is experiencing the lowest level of human life. As movement becomes purposeful action, a deliberate plan of some type begins to take place. This may be called a motivational action.*

• **THE DECISIVE MOMENT.** *Decision-making lies at the heart of any successful enterprise. A moment of decision and commitment must precede the motivational activities suggested in this book.*

HOW TO USE THIS BOOK

• **READ, MARK, NOTE, AND ACT.** *It used to be the custom to say of certain written documents that the reader had to read, mark, note and digest. Note the difference here. You do not **react** to this writing. You **act**. Read and act.*

• **A MANUAL RATHER THAN A TREATISE.** *This volume not only presents an idea but proposes a series of activities. It could be called a manual of action—a marriage maintenance manual.*

• **FOLLOW THE DECISIVE MOTIVATIONAL ACTION.** *Spaced throughout this volume are boxes headed "The Decisive Motivational Action." It's not enough just to read the book. You must do something about what you have read. Follow the suggested activities to put new zest and vitality into your marriage.*

Action Strategy #2

BEWARE—NO BARGAIN DIVORCES

"Till divorce us do part"

Two senior citizens were comparing some of their aches and pains when one of them remarked, "Getting old is terrible until you consider the alternative."

The same sentiment may be applied to marriage. With all the shortcomings of this human institution, the alternatives are worth considering. The most prevalent is divorce. But is divorce really a bargain or is the cure worse than the disease?

My father and mother had a shaky marriage. After ten stormy years, my father decided he'd had enough and walked out. For more than thirty years, until the day of his death, they were legally "separated" and lived apart with no intention of reconciliation. In those days there existed a few grounds for divorce which my mother could have used, but none available to my father. Through all these years he continued to pay alimony to my mother who looked upon this monthly payment as her "just" compensation for entering into a legal arrangement with my father.

In those days if one partner wanted to maintain the marriage, particularly if he or she were the "innocent" party, it was almost impossible to terminate the legal bond. Sometimes this situation leads to bargaining about terms under which the "innocent party" would give the "guilty" party his or her "freedom." Another way of resolving the whole matter was for the party who wanted out to obtain a "poor man's divorce" by simply running away and disappearing, a course of action not open to someone with roots down in a community.

How different today. Operating on the premise that no one should be required to remain in what is sometimes called a "loveless union" or a "life of slavery," a new concept has been introduced—"no-fault" divorce. No longer is it necessary to prove that one of the partners is "guilty." All that is needed is a conviction that a viable relationship no longer exists and it can be set aside.

Replacing the protracted legal procedures are not only "quickie" but also "cheapie" divorces with some attorneys setting up a standard rate with a kit available for "doing it yourself." For the really frugal, in some parts of the world, a postcard may be mailed in to terminate a marriage.

This new idea of "no-fault" divorce affects the whole institution of marriage in general; those involved in a marital relationship in particular.

It gets many a marriage off to a bad start. Kids enter marriage with the reservation, "If it doesn't work out, we'll just get a divorce." This attitude is in contrast to the days when marriage was a lifelong commitment and the partners looked toward a permanent lifelong relationship. This anticipation of the future often caused the prospective bride and groom to consider more carefully what they were getting into. Once married, they had a strong motivation to continue working at the relationship. Many people in such a marriage never dreamed of the possibility of divorce. However, one wife, in responding to the question as to whether she had ever thought of divorcing her husband said, "I've never ever considered divorcing him but I've often thought of murdering him!"

With the "new morality" has come a new attitude toward divorce. When the inevitable difficulties arise in marriage, instead of sticking at it and working it out, the young couple is tempted to call it off. They have a ready-made rationale for this attitude: "That's the way it is." "Marriage is like that." "It never works out." It takes a strong-minded young person to withstand these pressures and continue working at the relationship when modern divorce is an easy option. "Everybody's doing it!"

Divorce may be used as a weapon. An immature husband or wife may use the threat of divorce in much the same way that a child says, "If you don't play my way, I'll take my toys and go home."

Even worse, it is not unusual for a partner to file for a divorce and then as the proceedings get under way suddenly announce they have no desire to proceed with the action. Asked why the divorce was filed in the first place the answer sometimes is, "I just wanted to get his (her) attention." The trouble is the other partner may have now decided a divorce is a pretty good idea.

There is a good possibility wives will be the losers in a "no-fault" divorce. It has been estimated there are 3 million "displaced" homemakers in the U.S. today. This person is typically between the ages of 34 and 64, a woman who has been caring for family members and has lost her spouse through disability, death, or divorce. She may not have held a job for many years or never worked outside the home.

One displaced homemaker in her late fifties described her dilemma, "I was part of an invisible problem—too young for Social Security, too old to be hired, and not eligible for unemployment insurance because homemaking is not considered work."

Previously, a divorced wife could anticipate the alimony that came to the "innocent" party. Now even that option is disappearing. One of the debits from the new status of women is the expectation that a woman will go out and earn her own living. If her original life plans caused her to concentrate on being a wife and mother, it will probably mean she now lacks a marketable skill in the world of commerce. The higher her commitment to motherhood and the more years she has worked at being a wife and mother, the greater the probability she will be without the skills necessary to earn a living.

Discussing the no-fault divorce laws that have been adopted by forty-seven states, one feminine actionist notes that they are basically beneficial to younger women, but leave older women with no bargaining leverage and not enough to live on.

A divorced woman's financial security may be neither financially adequate nor secure. Studies reveal that while the economic status of former husbands improves, that of former wives deteriorates. Only two percent of all divorced women with children receive more than $5,000 a year in support. Only 14 percent of divorce settlements include any alimony, and only 44 percent award child support, but less than half of either is paid regularly. Moreover, if she finds employment, a working woman averages only 57 percent of a man's wages.

A study of the divorce laws in twenty-six countries by the International Social Security of Geneva showed that in most countries women lose Social Security benefits that have been determined by their husbands' earnings. In France, Belgium, and Austria a divorced woman loses her pension benefits, sickness, and maternity rights. It's patently unfair that the woman stands to be the financial loser but it is a reality that must be faced.

For a woman, remarriage will become a less viable option as she grows older. In part because of the greater longevity of women, the number of eligible marriage partners constantly decreases. There are more opportunities for a man to find a second partner. More women of all ages are available, plus it is acceptable for men to dip down into younger age brackets for female companionship. This is not true for the older female divorcee. If a man becomes interested in an older woman, his motives may be suspect. The greater the number of years a woman has spent in a marriage, the fewer are her possibilities for remarriage.

After a divorce, remarriage brings its own peculiar set of problems. The greater proportion of divorced people are candidates for remarriage. Most of them will try again. However, when a man has responsibility for child support, it cannot help but affect his relationship to his new wife. While the children of his former marriage may be his first financial priority, she may resent struggling with the problems of managing a budget haunted by the ghosts of the former family.

Other comparisons are inevitable. One wife was tactless enough to describe her first husband's sexual techniques as an example which thoroughly infuriated her new husband. He stated his position very clearly: "I'm not exactly a novice myself. I've been through two previous marriages and neither of my wives ever complained about my sexual techniques." They were both struggling with the legacy from the past that frequently complicates a new relationship.

"His" and "hers" (the children of previous marriages) may present the unique problem of a "blended" family.

The variety of combinations in the "blended" family is infinite. "Her" children may be living in the home while "his" children visit periodically, or vice versa. Children from both first marriages may be living under the same roof, offering a frustrating new form of sibling rivalry. And then there is always the possibility of "his," "hers," and "ours!" Some of these families work out, but many of them are an emotional mishmash that brings a tremendous potentiality for misunderstanding and conflict.

Children may be the major casualties in a divorce. Many divorces are "justified" on the basis that two ill-suited people will create an atmosphere detrimental to the children. When the divorce takes place, it is these very children who often come out on the losing end. A conversation with any school teacher will reveal that a large percentage of troublemakers in the classroom are products of a "broken home."

Children need a mother *and* a father. As Margaret Mead, noted anthropologist, used to say, "There is a need for new kinds of arrangements whereby no one can have children unless they can prove their ability to stay together—at least until the children are grown."

Parenthood is enormously complicated for the divorced. One woman writing of her own experiences said, "The world of the divorced woman with children is not glamorous. It is extremely difficult and overwhelming and the portrayal in movies, magazines, etc. too often does not show the reality of the situation. Divorce is a disaster and divorced mothers suffer from a tremendous overload. Sometimes I feel like I will lose my mind!"

For the man who elects to keep his children, the situation is considerably more complicated. Although he may have criticized his wife's child-rearing methods and become a hero to his kids, he now finds that holding down a full-time job and managing a home and children demands more than a 24-hour day.

One woman who chafed under the restraints of family life often fantasized the joys of living as a swinging single. Divorce seemed to offer the best of both worlds. She had custody of the children as well as her freedom. When she initiated her "free" life-style, she invited her new male friends to come to her home, only to discover that she was overwhelmed with fear that her children might discover what was going on. When they asked questions about the men who periodically visited the house, she had grave misgivings about this way of life.

Divorce may leave its own peculiar scars. Terminating a marriage that has not had a chance to grow and develop leaves the divorced man or woman with a sense of guilt and deep-seated inferiority. No matter how much the "no-fault" side of things is touted, there is always a sense of failure. As one woman put it, "When you marry you feel you have been chosen, and when the marriage is over you have a sense of having been 'unchosen'."

Divorce may rob you of years of life. While some have been rejoicing in their new freedom from the so-called "chains of marriage," we may need to consider some rather startling evidence indicating that divorce may have a physical effect on its subjects.

In his book, *The Broken Heart*, Lynch notes the effects of loneliness upon the incidence of heart disease. "It is a striking fact that U.S. mortality rates for all causes of death, not just heart disease, are consistently higher for divorced, single, and widowed individuals of both sexes and all races. Some of the increased death rates in unmarried individuals are astounding, rising as high as ten times the rates for married individuals of comparable ages."[1] This clinical psychologist further points out that such organizations as insurance companies that stake their money on projected life spans "have long recognized that a person's marital status is one of the best predictors of health, disease and death."[2] "A study carried out by Kitagawa and Hausek indicated that divorced males from 35 to 65 years of age had death rates 130 percent higher than married men while white female divorcees had a death rate 37 percent higher than that of married women."[3]

The point of Lynch's insightful book is that while most Americans are aware of the statistical evidence citing the effects of lack of exercise, diet, and smoking in heart disease, there is now equally convincing evidence to support loss of relationship as a contributing factor.

In a day when we are increasingly concerned about the environment and other agents that affect the length and quality of life, we need also to consider the effect of divorce on our life span.

Divorce may be destroying a national resource. Plato said it: "The life of the nation is but the life of the family writ large." If this is true, there is no more important civic duty than the conservation of this important institution that we call the family.

News has come of acts of vandalism that are enough to raise the hackles of even the most casual citizen. In the midst of a controversy between environmentalists and lumbermen over a proposed extension of the Redwood National Park, vandals attacked redwood trees with chain saws. Many of these majestic trees, some towering 300 feet into the sky, are more than a thousand years old. As the result of this attack with chain saws, nine of the trees were so badly damaged that they had to be felled.

In a few minutes the vandals had destroyed the growth of a thousand years. In felling the damaged trees, the rangers cut most of them close to the ground but left one large stump standing as "a sad reminder of what a maniac armed with a chain saw can do."

Like that pathetic stump stand the pathetic family units decimated by divorce. *Readers Digest* refers to this phenomenon as "War on the Family." Part of this attack takes the form of a new attitude toward marriage which says it is no longer to be considered a commitment to be kept but rather an agreement that can be put aside at will.

It has long been the practice of governments to recognize the value of families in strengthening national life. Many governments provide incentives for having children—baby bonuses, financial help with rearing children and, in England, has come a serious demand for wages for housewives. In contrast the U.S. has come up with a tax on marriage. As the income tax situation stands today, it is weighted in favor of people living together rather than making a marriage commitment. Take two couples both earning salaries; he earns $31,000 while she earns $9,000 for a combined annual income in each case of $40,000. If they decide to just live together and file separately, they will pay $7,215 income tax. Should they marry they will pay $7,427. Being married is penalized by $212 extra tax, instead of a tax on singles that is found in many countries.

Authorities hasten to assure us that the tax on marriage is an unfortunate oversight in the writing of the tax law. But the very fact that it could happen and that nothing has been done to correct the situation is evidence of a somewhat casual attitude toward the institution of marriage. Like those redwood stumps, many of our families stand today as mere shadows of their former selves and are affecting many aspects of national life in a large measure because of ease of divorce.

There is Another Way

If divorce holds so many dire possibilities, the sensible attitude will be to ask ourselves, "Is there another way?" It makes sense to sit down and explore some possible alternative procedures.

Writing an article on the subject of eating meals in a restaurant, the author opened with a twist: "One word of advice about taking the kids out to eat: Don't."

Similarly, my counsel to someone contemplating a divorce would be, "Don't. At least take time to weigh both the advantages and disadvantages. Don't do anything about your divorce until you have done something about your marriage!"

Start by taking a good hard look at divorce. Be realistic. Read the material in the box "Ten Ways A Divorce Lawyer Might Save Your Marriage." Then move on to the positive actions suggested in the following chapters.

Ten Ways A Divorce Lawyer Might Save Your Marriage

1. He can tell you precisely how much the divorce proceedings are going to cost. A divorce may amount to much more than you think!
2. He can explain the procedures for receiving alimony and point out the problems of collecting full or even partial payments.
3. Ask him how one gains custody of the children and some of the traumatic possibilities if both husband and wife are determined to get custody at any cost.
4. Discuss the matter of child support—how much and how long and what the alternatives are if your ex welches on his payments.
5. Discuss some of the problems of dividing the property—even such small things as the pots and pans, the linens, etc.
6. Let him tell you how you can contact him for your next divorce and the possibility that you will need his services again. Ask him about the percentage of clients who are repeaters.
7. Ask him to explain your rights in dealing with companies that withdraw your credit privileges after you are divorced.
8. Be sure you understand visitation rights and how to contend with an ex who wants the children at unusual times, spends money foolishly, and/or takes the opportunity to undermine you as a parent.
9. Consider the problems with your children's names when you remarry. Find out about adoption proceedings. Check on the cost.
10. Ask how he will feel if you have second thoughts about your divorce, particularly on the day it is to be granted.

Action Strategy #3

THINK AGAIN—WHAT DID YOU EXPECT?

*"She who waits for a knight in shining armor
may have to clean up after his horse."*

Ten years ago the U.S. Commissioner for Education announced a new educational goal for the world's most highly developed democracy—to eliminate illiteracy by 1980—a task which he described in the space-age goals of that day as "education's moon." Unfortunately, it seems as if the goal is still light-years away and that it has continued to recede into the distance. While most people may be able to read or write a simple message, when it comes to reading and writing enough to be a productive citizen living in a world of print, we are losing the battle. The number of functional illiterates continues to grow.

What has been called the "blight of illiteracy" is not confined to reading, writing and arithmetic. As important as are these skills in a modern society, even more necessary is the capacity to establish relationships with fellow humans, particularly those within marriage. Marital illiteracy abounds on every hand. Lacking basic relationship skills, people simply respond to basic biological urges and enter marriage with unreal expectations. Such marriages are doomed to failure before they begin.

Why do people marry? The question comes under a more searching scrutiny today than ever before. The reasons for marriage are many and varied.

The Jail-Break Marriage

Bonnie Rush was experiencing trouble in her marriage. "I know Joe is a wonderful person. He is so reliable, and I should be happy with him. But I married him for the wrong reason.

"In my late teens I had the feeling of being trapped in our family. I couldn't make a decision on my own. My mother was forever checking up on me and when I displeased my father, he talked to me like I was still a twelve-year-old. I began to wonder if I would ever become an independent person.

"Then along came Joe. Both of my parents liked him. He didn't look like much to me—rather ordinary, in fact. But in the back of my mind I thought, 'Here's my chance' and soon we were married. Now I have the same feeling as before. I'm stuck again. I want out."

This type of union is sometimes referred to as a jail-break marriage. The adolescent frequently sees the authoritarian father as warden and the overconcerned mother as jailer, both of whom seem determined that their prisoner will serve out a life sentence. The first man who comes along may become the convenient vehicle by which she can make her getaway.

Anne Harris also followed this route. When Philip Chappell began to ask her out, her reaction was, "He's not what I really want in a husband, but I can marry him, stay with him a decent time, and get a divorce. Then I can live my own life."

Anne had overlooked a simple biological fact. Shortly after the wedding she became pregnant. Now two desires battled within—independence and motherhood. When she first mentioned the pregnancy to her parents, they were so delighted with the prospect of becoming grandparents that Anne felt some real satisfaction. Soon after her initial joy at the birth, the dread, restrictive feeling closed in again. This time she had an added burden. She had jumped out of the frying pan into the fire.

A marriage of escape—from family, surroundings, school, or friends—may only result in a different form of entrapment.

The Tender Trap

Christian girls are in a particularly difficult situation when it comes to the sex issue. Just as much as her more permissive sister, she is aware of the stirring of sexuality within her and is subject to the same stimuli as other females. Moreover, in an enlightened Christian era she hears the emphasis that sex is good and creative. But along with this comes the message that sex is only to be experienced within the commitment and security of the marriage bond. As she becomes deeply involved in a relationship with a boy, perhaps accompanied by heavy petting sessions, marriage seems to be the only legitimate way to enjoy full sexual experience.

Judy Young was an attractive young lady growing up in a puritanical atmosphere. The boys she had always dated were courteous and considerate with her. But when Bob Davis appeared on the scene, his aggressive approach both attracted and overwhelmed her. One evening when her parents were away from home, after a long petting session, she yielded to Bob's entreaties and they went to bed together. In the midst of this encounter, her parents returned home.

Her father, infuriated, demanded that Davis do something to right this situation. Judy had misgivings about Bob Davis. But she sensed that she might now be "used goods." The marriage might just turn out all right. It would certainly give her release from the sexual tension of which she had become aware. Six months later, her new husband turned out to be so demanding and domineering that they finally divorced and she was forced into still another conflict—Is it right for a Christian to divorce?

Sexual satisfaction ought never to be the main reason for marriage. Sexual anticipations and appetites differ so widely that there is always the potentiality for conflict. By its very nature, sexual desire is cyclical—interest, developing desire, encounter, climax, loss of desire. A relationship based on sex alone will be in a state of continual fluctuation and lack constancy. Even if sexual relationships are of the highest order, sexual activity takes only a small portion of any given day. A lifelong commitment must depend upon other factors to foster the relationship.

The Safety Angle

Many girls still grow up with the fairy-tale illusion that some nice young man will come along and take care of them for the rest of their lives. For these, career goals are secondary and, having husband-hunted their way through school, may come out with no clear-cut ambitions outside of marriage. By the senior year of college, panic sets in. If a bright, young man who seems to be going someplace happens along at this time—he doesn't have a chance! In the past, this has been the technique by which many pretty girls have achieved status and security.

Men may be just as susceptible to this kind of motivation for marriage. Neal Tidwell expressed the sentiment: "I guess I needed someone to take care of me. I had moved into an apartment, but keeping house was a continuous hassle. The girl across the hall wasn't particularly attractive, but she cooked, cleaned and ran her apartment with an efficiency that rivaled that of my mother. I was delighted when she offered to help me." He received a promotion which involved moving to another state and began planning his move. As he discussed his plans with Betty, it was a small step to suggesting they might marry and she could come with him. Once married, Betty was no longer willing to be a "household drudge."

And what about the insecure man who seeks his security through an aggressive female? Rugged, handsome but not too energetic or highly motivated man meets capable, driving ambitious girl. Opposites attract. Result: marriage. He is satisfied, at least temporarily, to fulfill his ambitions vicariously.

While she climbs the corporate ladder or gets her graduate degree, he takes the "easy way out" and cares for the routine responsibilities. That is, until he begins to resent her "success" and his own self-imposed image. (Note: This is not to be confused with the current trend in cooperative home management. The term "house husband" has been coined to identify the new breed of marriage wherein, by mutual agreement, the husband and wife reverse roles for a period of time in order to better understand their partner's point of view.)

Two Can Live As Cheaply As One

Getting an education is often a long and costly business.

Frequently, large sums of money must be borrowed to be repaid later. Student marriages often encounter severe financial stress. The marriage may begin on the basis that "two can live as cheaply as one" and she will go on with her education while they both continue their part-time jobs. Then comes the time when she drops out of school "temporarily" while he gets his degree and she must settle for a P.H.T. (putting hubby through). As time goes by she grows more and more frustrated about missing her opportunity to complete her education. It is even more ironic when he decides she hasn't "kept up with him" and seeks a divorce.

When Opportunity Knocks

Traditionally, a girl has seen the members of her sex fulfilling two primary roles—that of wife and mother. Even in our enlightened age, the subtle message to females still may be, "You are who you marry and whom you mother." An indication of her first accession is that she will be known by her husband's name "Mrs. John Wilson" or when the children come along, as "Jerome Wilson's mother."

As she becomes aware of the rhythms of her own body, she realizes they periodically repeat the message of her child-bearing function. To become a mother, she needs a husband not only to father her children but also to stand by and care for her.

Hetty Wesley was an example of this traditional role of woman. At the ripe old age of 27, she was still not married. Her father disapproved of the man with whom she eloped, only to be deserted shortly thereafter. When she returned home pregnant, her father insisted on immediate marriage. Brilliant Hetty offered herself as a bride to whoever would take her and married an ignorant villager.

Lest we think Hetty's experience was a phenomenon of the eighteenth century, we might note that something like 50 percent of today's teenage brides get married because they are pregnant. Many of these might never have married if it had not been for the pregnancy. The argument is, "We were going to marry, anyway. This just hurried things up a little." Yet, whenever there is a pregnant bride, there is built-in stress and a lot of questions. The most compelling question is, "Would we have really married if she had not been pregnant?"

Partly because of the cultural background of our society, the male generally proposes to the female. This has left some girls in a difficult position. One very capable woman when asked why she had not married simply answered, "No one ever asked me." A girl approaching her thirtieth year is often subjected to a subtle but cruel torture as well-meaning friends and relatives ask, "Aren't you married yet?" The situation is aggravated by the knowledge that the field of eligible males is constantly narrowing. A normally cool-headed girl may panic and enter into a less than satisfactory relationship.

Falling In Love

Of all the strange experiences that overtake human beings there is none more perplexing than that which is described as "falling in love." The Greeks who gave us the original words for love sometimes described the reaction as "madness." A person in the throes of romantic love could easily be described as neurotic or even psychotic. Some of these symptoms of romantic love are:

1. Love is a dramatic and often unexpected experience which suddenly overtakes its victim.
2. Being "in love" may distort the judgment of the individual.

3. Love is a never-ending quest with the love object always evading the lover's grasp.
4. Being in love is preeminently an experience of the emotions.
5. The experience of romantic love is often most irrational.
6. The experience of love may immobilize the "victim."
7. A lover may be so preoccupied with thoughts of his beloved that the state could only be adequately described as an obsession.
8. There are evidences of a well-formed delusional system in some romantic love encounters.

And such a state often leads to marriage!

Thus it happens that the dating period before marriage which should be a testing time is frequently marred by the attitude of two people who look at each other through rose-colored glasses. "He's all I ever hoped a man might be!" "She is the most wonderful girl in the world!" And during courtship days this may partly be true.

The behavior modifiers tell us that the way to establish desirable behaviors is to give them attention, and the highest form of attention is praise. Two people looking into each other's eyes and continually commending one another are bound to give and receive euphoria.

Following marriage, there comes a saturation point and a new attitude may emerge. This is summarized in the law of Pre- and Post-Marital Perceptions: "Before marriage the loved one's virtues are perceived and faults are overlooked. Following marriage, faults are magnified and virtues overlooked."

One of the problems may be the sequence in which we westerners place marriage. A wedding is viewed as the consummation of a long period of preliminary activity. Rather like climbing a mountain, the lovers struggle till they reach the peak (marriage) then sit down to enjoy the view. But in cultures where parents choose the partner, the new husband and wife realize marriage is just a beginning and they are entering upon a new relationship at which they will have to work.

In the musical, *Fiddler on the Roof*, Tevye reminds his wife, Golde, that the first time they met was *on their wedding day*. Their parents had told them that they would *learn* to love each other. For them marriage began at the foot of the mountain—not at its crest. Together, they climbed slowly, learning to work together as a team, struggling to overcome obstacles, making their way toward the pinnacle. Consequently, the activity brought its own rewards.

This approach is compatible with Dr. Karl Menninger's formulation on the subject of love: "One does not 'fall' in love: one *grows* into love and love grows in him."[1] Love at its best is a gradual growing process.

If romantic love is the basis for marriage, there may come a "falling out of love" which may be perceived as a reason for divorce. One cynic has come up with an evaluation of the romantic love syndrome, "She who waits for a knight in shining armor must clean up after his horse."

The success of the "Playboy Philosophy" which views women as sex objects existing to fulfill the somewhat adolescent sexual fantasies of American males is anti-woman and anti-family.

However, in a recent poll conducted by a prominent publication surveying the values, attitudes, and goals of American males aged 18 to 49, the surprising findings included some of the following:

• Eighty-five percent of the men described "family life" as being very important to them; almost two-thirds of the men stated that their own family lives were "very satisfactory."

• Married men expressed greater sexual satisfaction with their lives than single men.

•Three out of four of the respondents said that they considered sexual fidelity for both males and females to be "very important" for the success of a marriage.

•Less than half (49 percent) of the men labeled sex as "very important" to their personal happiness.

• Asked their reasons for marrying, 74 percent specified "having another person to share one's life," and 62 percent "having someone to share life's experiences with." Only 27 percent married "to have a steady sex life."

A professional newsletter reporting the findings referred to them as *The Unsexy Results!*

If you married to escape from an irksome home situation, to find sexual fulfillment, to make life secure, to take advantage of an opportunity, or because you fell in love, you may have gotten off to a bad start. Remember the words of the sales manager to his salesmen, "It's not what the customer comes in for that counts, it's what he goes out with that's important."

If marriage is an activity rather than a state, it's not what you set out to get, but what you are willing to do about it. In the following chapters you will find some ideas to help you discover just where you are, where you want to be, and some steps toward arriving at a happier marital condition.

Action Strategy #4

PUT IT DOWN IN BLACK AND WHITE

*"Sanctity of contract is the basis of modern
business life."*

One point of discussion that periodically arises in discussions with sexually-aware adolescents is the importance of a marriage commitment in a relationship between two people. The popular argument heard more and more often is, "What difference does a piece of paper make? It's the relationship that counts! Why should we have to go through the form dictated by the state and/or the church?"

What difference does a piece of paper make?

Apply the same principle to the totality of life. One title company has a logo of two people standing together with the inscription, "Sanctity of contract is the basis of modern business life." Where would we be without automobile titles, land deeds, memoranda of agreements, death certificates, and drivers' licenses?

At the outbreak of World War II, when Imperial Germany ignored the agreement not to invade neutral

Belgium, the excuse offered by the aggressors was that the agreement was "only a scrap of paper." Ignoring that "scrap of paper" plunged the world into the most serious conflict of human history up to that time. A piece of paper signed by people of goodwill can be very important.

Not only the legality of the transaction but also the unreliability of human memory enters into the situation. As a result in part from the high cost of writing a letter these days (about $6.00 per letter), plus the strange tendency of the postal service to be somewhat less than efficient in getting said letter to its destination, many companies are using the telephone for business. Whereas the advertisements formerly called upon the responder to fill in a coupon and forward it to the advertiser, now the instructions are to call a toll-free number.

While these verbal methods of communication have all the advantages of speed and economy, they are lacking in one area—keeping a record of the agreement. The written word provides a record.

My mother certainly believed in the power of the written word. One vivid memory of boyhood days was running errands to the store. My Australian mother referred to these errands as "messages," and in many ways the message was the heart of the process. As a small lad I was given to daydreaming and easily diverted from my task by the side attractions I encountered along the way. Consequently, when I arrived at the store, I had forgotten what I was to buy!

My mother adopted a time-honored technique. She wrote out the "message" on a piece of paper, carefully wrapped the money in it, placed it all in an envelope, and then with a long safety pin affixed the whole thing inside my shirt pocket. When I arrived at the store the storekeeper reached over and unfastened the "message" with the money enclosed. After reading the note, filling the order, and making the change, he placed it inside the envelope and repinned it to my shirt pocket.

My mother had hit upon what management specialist Charles E. Redfeld has concluded about the business world: "The written word is not distortion-proof, but it suffers less from distortion over a period of time or in a lengthy channel than does its oral counterpart."

Signing on the Dotted Line

Thomas Maxwell, an executive of Vanguard Products, is conferring with Ralph Unwin about his M.B.O.'s (Management By Objective). Ralph is discussing the objectives that he has written out stating exactly what he hopes to accomplish in the coming year. After a good deal of discussion, Ralph and his superior reach a conclusion as to the realistic, viable aims that Ralph may expect to reach. There is a sense in which his M.B.O.'s are a contract with his immediate superior whereby both parties understand just what he will be attempting to do in the next twelve months.

This principle is being used by many engaged couples who sit down together before marriage and spell out in black and white exactly what each will expect to give and receive in their marriage relationship. Working out written goals for a marriage helps to clarify the expectations of both partners. These are generally of three types:

1. Goals which can be discussed freely between a prospective husband and wife.
2. Goals of which the couple are aware but may feel reluctant to discuss at this time.
3. Ideals tucked away in the subconscious which may periodically surface.

The obvious place to start is with the goals that can be freely discussed. Once these have been aired and conclusions reached, they are written down. By now the more sensitive issues at the secondary level will be considerably defused. After these have been put on the table, those vague hopes tucked away in the unconscious can be mentioned. This process is sometimes referred to as "peeling the skin off the onion." As successive layers are peeled away, new layers become evident.

Report has it that when Jackie Kennedy and Aristotle Onassis planned their marriage, they drew up a 170-point premarital marriage contract covering every possible detail of their married life. For more normal humans, however, the contract will be much simpler and cover the more concrete issues relating to the marriage relationship.

Maureen and Don Pickford's Premarital Contract

1. *Maureen elects to be known as Mrs. Maureen Pickford and wishes to use this name legally rather than Mrs. Don Pickford.*

2. *Because we do not want to have children immediately, we will practice birth control, deciding on the method in cooperation with our physician. In our planning each will accept responsibility.*

3. *At this time we both agree we will ultimately have children. However, we will not start our family until we have been married for at least a year. We will plan to have two children spaced by at least eighteen months. If for any reason, we cannot have children of our own, we will attempt to adopt.*

4. *Responsibility for rearing the children will rest upon the shoulders of both Maureen and Don and they will be*

> *reared in the Christian faith. Both of us pledge to set the example in our Christian commitment and church attendance.*
>
> 5. *We will both work for the first year of marriage and will decide on a place of residence nearest to the place of employment.*
> 6. *While Maureen works outside the home, all housework will be shared equally as far as possible.*
> 7. *We will pool all income. After expenses are deducted, each will have spending money with any surplus going into a joint account.*
> 8. *This contract will be renegotiated on or about August 15, approximately one year from today.*

A good premarital contract would spell out action in the following areas:

1. Where will the couple live?
2. What will be the relationship with parents? How frequently will they see them?
3. What about religion? What church will they attend? How frequently?
4. How about family planning? What technique of birth control will they use?
5. How about children? How soon after marriage? If necessary, will they adopt?
6. How will the children be brought up? By what guidelines?
7. Will the wife work? Any stated period of time?
8. What plan of money management will be used? Will one partner be responsible as treasurer?

Obviously, these are elementary facts of married life. Unfortunately, however, many young couples enter into marriage without having realistically faced some of the areas where problems are most likely to arise.

We have already mentioned Thomas Maxfield discussing his M.B.O.'s (Management By Objective) with his boss. To set up objectives is one thing; to fulfill them, another. So in some stated period of time, say a year later, the boss and his executive sit down and review the results of the year's work. What happened? Were the objectives realized? Were they unrealistic? Should they write a new set of objectives?

Renegotiating a Contract

As married life goes on, the relationship will pass through a number of fairly well-defined stages. Each of these will probably bring situations that could not have been anticipated at the outset of a marriage relationship.

The Associated Press reported an unusual experiment. In an unguarded moment the husband, a high school football coach, downgraded his wife's complaints about the difficulties of running the house for a husband and family of two boys and two girls. He remarked that housework was child's play and she wouldn't last long in the "real" world of work. As a result of this discussion, they agreed that the wife would go back to work while her husband would stay home and care for the family. They prepared what was called a "Motherhood Contract" and had it duly notarized. This document spelled out the terms of the seventy-day experiment of role reversal, specifying the responsibilities and privileges of both husband and wife.

Although accustomed to the pressures of coaching a high school football team, the coach soon discovered he couldn't stand up to the rigors of caring for four children ranging in age from four to sixteen! The straw that broke the camel's back came one day as he was cleaning house. "The kids were fighting over a TV program and smearing their fingerprints on my clean windows. My back was sore from vacuuming and in frustration, I blurted: 'Just wait till your mother gets home!' "

He couldn't believe his own words. *What did I just say?*

With two days remaining in his contract, he hung up his apron and dish towel, proclaiming, "I have come to the conclusion there is no profession, career, or occupation on earth which parallels motherhood in either degree of difficulty or importance of outcome relative to the future success of the world."

The event was so traumatic to the coach that he confessed, "I believe my failure as a mother could be construed by many (mothers) as the greatest success since Adam took a bite out of Eve's apple."

With the wife the situation was different. She enjoyed being away from the house, fitting neatly into a niche as a secretary. She was not so sure that the experiment had failed. The upshot was that the husband and wife sat down together for a prolonged session of renegotiation. Because of his aversion to housework and her satisfaction with her new role, they finally reached a compromise. She would work part-time as a secretary and he would share the household chores.

The virtues of a contract are also its vices. Putting it down in black and white makes the agreement specific and definite, but it should not be "the law of the Medes and Persians." A written contract provides an excellent starting point but it should be periodically reviewed so that it becomes a guideline rather than a straight jacket.

A Reaffirmation

Marriage involves paperwork. It begins when two people sign a certificate in which they make their initial marriage commitment to each other. It concludes with another piece of paper. This may be a divorce decree or a death certificate. Between these two points there is a place for some sort of new commitment along the way.

One such document is the "give and take" contract. Such an exercise enables a husband and wife to do some negotiating. It is built on the premise that both a husband and wife are willing to give as well as take from their marriage. The couple involved fill out a form with two columns headed "What I Want from This Marriage" and "What I Am Willing to Contribute to This Marriage." Under these headings both parties list what they want and what they are willing to give.

In order for this exercise to be effective, it is important that the parties learn to write detailed descriptive statements:

NOT: "I want you to cooperate."
BUT: "I want you to hear me out when I try to tell you something."

Similarly when stating the expectations one has from the marriage, it must be spelled out specifically:

NOT: "I want you to respect me."
BUT: "When we meet somebody, I want you to introduce me."

Such revealing statements should lead to discussion of the behaviors concerned. Details of a similar process will be discussed in a later chapter of this book.

I recently heard of an interesting wedding. The parties had been married for thirty years. To celebrate their thirtieth anniversary, they decided to be remarried. They invited their children and friends and had a reception. Officiating at the ceremony was the clergyman who had performed the original wedding ceremony.

For a couple who have seriously decided to put some new life into their marriage, such an experience could be appropriate. Along with the second marriage ceremony could go a second marriage contract that would form the basis for a new married life.

At the culmination of a long and distinguished career in law, 81-year-old Paul P. Ashley produced a volume entitled *Oh Promise Me, but Put It in Writing*. In this book he presents a plausible case for written contracts in a marriage relationship. From his wide legal background he asks, "What astute person would consider it sensible to decide on an important business transaction while parked romantically beside a moonlit lake?" Yet, this is the way most decisions about marriage are made. Ashley makes a strong point, "There is a tendency to live up to a written promise or at least make an effort to do so—when one might shrug off an oral commitment as mere conversation, the specifics of which are long since forgotten."[1]

Our Second Marriage Contract

I AGREE that I really am interested in preserving our marriage and I will listen to any practical suggestion you have whereby I can improve my conduct toward this goal. I know I am far from perfect, and I will welcome any constructive advice that may help me fulfill myself.

I AGREE to be as honest with both you and myself as I possibly can be. I will withhold no information about my behavior, either before or since we married. You have full right to know the person you married.

I AGREE that I will listen to your remarks and comments without interrupting you. When it is my turn to talk, I expect the same courtesy.

I AGREE that I will first look for things to criticize about myself before I criticize you. Before I complain to you, I will name some fault of mine that, if corrected, would make me a better marriage partner.

I AGREE to cooperate in writing out a list of specific family goals that I am willing to support—and I agree to accept responsibility for doing anything and everything I can to help achieve those goals.

I AGREE to cooperate in working out a realistic family budget. I will do my best to accept full responsibility for living within that budget.

I AGREE not to expect miracles in the improvement of our marriage. There is a great deal you need to know about me and I about you before we can consider ourselves truly married. But I will make every effort toward mutual knowledge and understanding.

I AGREE, on the assumption that example is the most persuasive form of argument known to man, that I will diligently seek to improve myself so I can grow into a continually better model of a marriage mate.

HE _____

SHE _____

DATE _____

The Decisive Motivational Action

Why not try putting it down in black and white? Instead of feeling irritated about some of your spouse's behaviors, use the "What I Want" and "What I Am Willing To Give" technique.

Prepare two sheets of paper with the headings shown below. The husband should fill out one and the wife the other.

Remember to use behavioral terms in describing what you want and what you are willing to give.

NOT: *"I want my husband to love me."*

BUT: *"I would like my husband to tell me he loves me at least once a day."*

NOT: *"I want to be proud of my wife."*

BUT: *"I would like my wife to lose ten pounds."*

WHAT I WANT FROM THIS MARRIAGE	WHAT I AM WILLING TO CONTRIBUTE TO THIS MARRIAGE

After you have completed this exercise, exchange papers. Think it over for a couple of days. Then arrange a time when you can sit down together for discussion.

Can you come to a compromise agreement?

Action Strategy #5

REDUCE RESENTMENT

"Deciding that our freedom is worth more than our resentments, we are using that Power to help us free ourselves from these resentments."

Seven Steppers

When a professional in the field of marital relationship appears before a lay audience, one question is inevitable, "What is the single most important problem faced by husbands and wives today?"

The audience waits for the answer, "Sex, finances, in-law difficulties, management of the children . . ."

Of course it is one of those unanswerable questions that always leads me to recall the question asked George Bernard Shaw, "If you were wrecked on a desert island and could only have one book, what would it be?"

The anticipated answer was the Bible, Shakespeare's plays or some other similar volume, but the irascible Irishman replied, "I'd take Smith's *Practical Guide to Shipbuilding*."

However, if I were compelled to answer a question about marital relationships I'd take the plunge and say unhesitatingly, "The resentment syndrome."

Some of my fellow professionals might answer, "The what?"

Resentment is seldom talked about. Virtually no books have been written on the subject, and an examination of the indexes of books on marriage counseling shows they, too, are strangely silent.

The one group of workers with a lot to say on the subject is the leaders of self-help groups. These non-professionals working very effectively with some of the most stubborn personality problems like alcoholism, drug addiction and criminal propensities see some of the greatest struggles in the area of resentment.

It may be that one reason why professionals have said so little about resentment is that resentment is not easily described. It is not just a single entity but rather a whole group of related reactions that could more accurately be described as a syndrome. The resentment syndrome is a combination of reactions representing some of the most destructive forces attacking marriage relationships today.

The Invisible Wall

Marriage is primarily an experience of union and affiliation. The biblical equation is $1 + 1 = 1$; one man plus one woman equals one flesh. The Bible lays down the ideal that a man leaves his father and mother to cleave to his wife. The word *cleave* means "to bond," "to glue." Resentment is just the opposite—a lever that separates, pries people apart, and divides.

Few sights are more chilling than the wall that divides East from West Germany. Built by the East Germans—not to keep the enemy out, but to keep their own people in—it stands as a silent monument to the tyranny of Marxism.

On one occasion I stood in a border observation post looking through binoculars into East German territory. I was aware that the East German soldiers had us under constant observation from their concrete tower. Never was "big brother" more realistically present in my life. But it was at Check Point Charlie, the entrance into the city of East Berlin, that the wall seemed so sickeningly real. That wall had snaked through a city, dividing houses, neighbors and even families. For many years families were unable even to visit each other. Wreaths hanging on the wall in memory of would-be escapees shot down while trying to scale the wall gave mute evidence of its effectiveness in keeping people apart.

The wall of resentment, though not visible to the eye, is just as effective a barrier in many families, as was seen with John and Ruth Groves. Although they appeared to have a good marriage on the surface, they lived with an underlying conflict over their sex life. John had a healthy sex drive, while Ruth's sexual interest was at a low level. She participated in sexual activity mainly out of wifely obligation.

As the years passed Ruth managed to get across the message to John that he was oversexed. After several encounters in which Ruth made some cutting remarks about John "raping" her and being "animalistic," they settled into separate bedrooms. John spent more and more time away from the home until there came a day when Ruth suddenly realized they had only a shadow of a marriage. In desperation she made an appointment to see a counselor and persuaded John to come with her.

At the counseling session John had plenty to say. While he wasn't planning to terminate the marriage at this time, he gave some broad hints that once the children were grown, he would reevaluate his situation. He made a number of sarcastic references to Ruth's unfortunate use of words *rape* and *animal*. Informed that Ruth was anxious to rebuild the relationship, he responded, "I'm sorry but there is such a wall between us that I don't see any possibility of doing that."

The wall he was referring to was the wall of resentment. Two people can live in the same house, walk the same carpets, and even sleep in the same bed, yet have an invisible wall between them. This wall has been built a block at a time through the years from resentments which have arisen in the relationship and now stand as a solid barrier to real communication.

Looking the Wrong Way

Interesting that John Graves should recall some of his wife's statements from the past. The essence of resentment is a constant reference to something that happened earlier.

Angel Sparkman was also vividly aware of the past. Her husband, Al, was the eternal optimist—particularly at the card table. Gambling had always held a strange fascination for him. When his company sent him to a convention at Las Vegas, he took with him the $5,000 he and Angel had saved to remodel their house. Of course, he had not bothered to mention the matter to Angel. Like so many other wooers of Lady Luck, he lost it all. He didn't tell Angel for some weeks, and when she finally saw the bank statement and demanded to know the whereabouts of the money, he tried to excuse himself by saying he might have easily doubled their capital.

As much as they tried they never could accumulate that much money again. Consequently, the remodeling was postponed. As Angel watched her friends moving into their new houses or remodeling their old homes, she became the more frustrated. As she expressed it,

"Whenever we have a difference and start arguing, I immediately think of Al's irresponsibility at Las Vegas. It doesn't matter what we talk about, it all leads straight back to Las Vegas."

There are many illustrations that can be used of the married state, but I think I like best the one evoked by the old song "Daisy" in which marriage is seen as a husband and wife riding a bicycle built for two. Perhaps this nostalgic song led my wife and me to buy a tandem bike. When we mount that bicycle to go for our daily ride, we are a sight to behold. Warmup suits, shoes, helmets and on the side of my spectacles—a tiny mirror. I hate wearing glasses. I only need them for reading. But when riding the bike I wear them so I will have something to which to fit my miniature mirror. That little rear-view mirror is worn in an effort to cope with a major cycling problem—looking back. While taking an eye off the ball may cause a missed tennis shot or a strike in baseball, it is nothing compared with what may happen to a cyclist who tries to look around at what is going on behind him.

Backward looks in the marriage relationship can be equally dangerous. The word *resentment* comes from two Latin words and literally means "to feel back." It can usher in a crippling marital condition.

The apostle Paul exhorted the Philippian Christians to look ahead and "Forgetting those things which are behind . . . reaching forth unto those things which are before I press toward the mark for the prize of the high calling" (Phil. 3:13-14, KJV).

Like California running back, Roy Riegels, who charged down the football field only to discover he had run the wrong way and paved the way for the opposing team's victory, moving in the wrong direction can mean losing in the game of marriage.

Imprisoned

Let's face it, resentment is self-defeating. The Seven Steppers certainly understand this self-defeating aspect of the reaction. This organization was founded by Bill Sands, son of a California judge. An ex-convict himself, Sands has majored on rehabilitating convicts by group experiences in the pre- and post-release period of prison life.

Appropriately for convicts, their program of action is stated in the form of an acrostic formed around the word FREEDOM:

1. F acing the truth about ourselves and the world around us, we decided we need to change.
2. R ealizing that there is a Power from which we can gain strength, we have decided to use that Power.
3. E valuating ourselves by taking an honest self-appraisal, we examined both our strengths and our weaknesses.
4. E ndeavoring to help ourselves overcome our weaknesses, we enlisted the aid of that Power.
5. D eciding that our freedom is worth more than our resentments, we are using that Power to help us free ourselves from these resentments.
6. O bserving that a daily program is necessary, we set an attainable goal toward which we could work each day.
7. M aintaining our own freedom, we pledge ourselves to help others as we have been helped.

In many ways, the crux of the program of Seven Steppers is contained in the fifth step: "Deciding that our freedom is worth more than our resentments, we are using that Power to help us free ourselves from these resentments."

Resentment presents a major problem for the convict. Leaving prison with a chip on his shoulder, he is vulnerable, overreacts, makes an impulsive move, gets in trouble with the law, and finishes up back in the penitentiary once again. The person who nurses resentments is just as much a prisoner as the inhabitant of any penitentiary. The main difference is the nature of the prison. Rather than stones and mortar, resentment is an emotional wall which just as effectively incarcerates the subject.

Getting Even

When Donna Humphreys discovered that her husband, Jim, had been involved in a questionable relationship with his secretary, she was furious. Jim quickly acknowledged his foolish mistake and asked his wife's forgiveness. Donna, anxious to maintain the marriage, was nevertheless humiliated and let him know her feelings in no uncertain terms. She did not want to divorce Jim, but the memory of what he did rankled her and she devised a way to take revenge.

To justify her action, she built a rationale in her mind. She reasoned, "Why did Jim seek this experience? Maybe I was an inadequate lover, and he went off seeking someone with wider experiences." So she began to look around. As she told about it later she said, "I had a need for some man to want me. I didn't care whether it was the newsboy or the plumber just as long as a man found me desirable." So working on the basis of what's good for the gander is good for the goose, she became involved in a torrid affair that erupted in a whole series of complications. Later, she admitted she never really enjoyed those sexual escapades. She really just wanted to get even with Jim.

Getting even has always had a certain appeal. But revenge can be a hollow victory. It flies in the face of the teaching of Jesus who urged his followers to turn the other cheek, forgive their enemies, bless those who cursed them, and love the people who hated them. He also said that if an individual refused to forgive another, he would not be forgiven himself which leaves the resentful person in a dubious spiritual condition.

Battered Mates

It comes as something of a shock to the beginning student of human behavior to discover that the most intimate of all human experiences between man and woman— sexual intercourse—which should be the expression of love and tenderness, is sometimes associated with cruelty, punishment, and suffering. Experts in the field of human sexuality speak about the sado-masochistic reaction in which men and women gain pleasure by punishing or receiving punishment from a partner. Evidence for the prevalence of this behavior is seen in the widespread dissemination of pornographic materials portraying activities referred to in their vernacular as bondage and discipline which are really sado-masochistic.

From the beginning point of punishment and pain leading to sexual gratification, the concept has been extended to people receiving any sort of pleasure from either inflicting or receiving pain, particularly in husband-wife relationships. The classical case is seen in the publicized instances of battered wives. Some observers claim that, in many of these cases, the experience may be seen as a marital interaction in which the husband gets his satisfaction from beating his wife and the wife experiences a certain gratification from being the victim.

But punishment doesn't have to take a physical form. The most devastating type of punishment may be mental or emotional. This sado-masochistic component is clearly seen in the resentment syndrome where a resentful person gets a peculiar satisfaction out of either suffering at the hands of or punishing a mate.

The mechanism may take another form as seen in the case of Keith Mitchell. Keith had become involved in an affair with a girl he met while bowling. The whole thing was somewhat superficial and when his wife, Mavis, told him about the rumors she had heard, he readily acknowledged a foolish flirtation and asked Mavis' forgiveness.

Mavis was scared at first, but once she regained her composure she began to see ways she could get some mileage from the situation. She insisted on Keith recounting the whole event for her. No detail was too small. She insisted that he go back over it again and again, meanwhile breaking into tears at appropriate spots and pointing out how cruelly he had treated her. She became the super martyr.

The sadistic side of the symptom is seen in the psychic torture through which one partner will put a spouse. Tim Anderson was a rather rigid no-nonsense young man preparing for the ministry. His intensity of purpose caused him to neglect his wife, Hazel. He justified his attitude to her by insisting that when he had completed his seminary training, they'd have time to get their marriage together. To maintain their home, it was necessary for Hazel to work. She found employment in an office where the youthful boss was a kind and understanding man. Attracted to him, Hazel got in deeper than she intended. Then in a remorseful reaction, she left her job and told her husband.

When they went to see a counselor, Tim objected strenuously to the suggestion that he wait outside while the counselor talked with Hazel. When they came together after the interview, Tim insisted Hazel go back over the details again. It soon became clear he was immensely enjoying the tears of his penitent wife, particularly in the presence of the counselor, and intended to punish her for what she had done.

The sado-masochistic reaction is unhealthy and indicates another way in which a resentment can further damage a marriage relationship.

Reactive or Proactive?

Possibly the most frustrating single aspect of resentment is that it seems life is out of our own hands and under the control of someone else. Gordon Allport, one of the most illustrious psychologists America has produced, has charged his fellow psychologists with being forever occupied with the "re" words—*reflex, reaction, response*—words indicating a passive condition. This troubled psychologist suggested the time had come for an emphasis on the "pro" words—*programming, proceeding, promise.* Resentment is life lived at the reactive level.

Doctors have long noted the way our emotions affect our bodies. The manner in which we react to others may be an action of self-destruction. The noted eighteenth-century Scottish physician, John Hunter, who suffered from angina pectoris, once remarked, "My life is in the hands of any rascal who chooses to annoy and tease me." Ironically, he predicted the precise circumstances of his own death. One day at a medical board meeting, Hunter got into an argument with a colleague who had contradicted him. He became so enraged that he stormed out of the room and immediately dropped dead. But why put our lives into someone else's hands? We should take control of our own affairs. We need to become *proactive* rather than *reactive*.

A famous mother of the eighteenth century had remarkable success in raising the ten of her children who survived to adulthood. On one occasion she wrote a letter to her son telling him about her method of raising and teaching the children. Among the many choice statements which this wise woman made concerning her rules for managing the children is one that should be written in ten-foot letters:

"ONCE A FAULT HAS BEEN CONFESSED, IT WILL NOT BE MENTIONED AGAIN."

Not bringing up the past is a simple rule that could transform husband-wife relationships and open up a new era of living in family life.

Mastering Runaway Emotions

One of the most devastating aspects of the resentment experience is the way runaway emotions overwhelm us and defeat the rational processes so important for viable family living. Some homes are like those of the people living in the Snake River Valley who were farming the fertile land when the huge earthen Teton Dam collapsed and washed away everything in its pathway.

Alethia Murray knew all about rampant floods of another type. Expecting her second child at 39 years of age, she was justly apprehensive. Just three weeks from the anticipated delivery date, her husband, Harry, came home with the news that the boss wanted him to take some clients to their hunting lodge in Canada for a few days. Harry kept assuring her that there was no way that the baby could come early. It was pretty clear to her that he really wanted to go on this hunting trip. Alethia agreed reluctantly and the day after his departure went into a hard and difficult labor. It was a nightmarish experience. Just at the moment when she needed him most, Harry was hunting in Canada!

Alethia just could not forget those terrible days. As she related, "I know all the reasons why I should forget about this incident. I'm aware that any mention of it will only hurt my relationship with my husband. But some foolish little thing will spark the memory—a word, a name, a sound and my head becomes like a movie, one scene after the other. Then, before you can turn around, I am pouring out my hostility and reminding him of all the details of the thing we both desperately need to forget."

Never underestimate the power of emotions. Psychologists speak about affective disorders when describing the vulnerability of human personality to emotional attacks. In trying to describe the problems that beset human beings, we recognize one of the most devastating of these as "emotional illness." In another chapter we will consider the vulnerability of humans to the onslaught of emotions, but here it is necessary to note that the chink in the armor through which emotions may attack us is the resentment syndrome.

Handling the Resentment Syndrome

The resentment syndrome calls for decisiveness. The philosopher Kant discovered that his trusted servant, Lampe, had systematically robbed him over a period of years. Although he needed Lampe desperately, he discharged his servant and wrote in his journal, "Remember to forget Lampe."

Miss Clara Barton, the founder of the American Red Cross, also learned this lesson. A friend of Miss Barton asked her about a particularly traumatic event in her life. Miss Barton seemed perplexed.

"Can't you remember?"

Miss Barton replied, "I distinctly remember forgetting it."

Like the little Dutch boy who put his finger in the dike to stop the water from eroding the barrier away, so we need to go into action to prevent erosion by resentment.

Alethia Murray, the resentful mother, talked her problem over with a psychologist and they decided to use the "Stop-Think" technique. She procured a card headed "Resentment Reducer." On this card she stated her problem.

1. "Harry was hunting when I needed him most."
2. She thinks of six good points about Harry.

Alethia carries the card in her pocketbook, and the moment the old thought enters her mind, Alethia goes into action.

a. Removes the card and looks at it.
b. Concentrates on STOP—says it out LOUD—if convenient, SHOUTS!
c. Reads and concentrates on six good points about Harry.

The psychologist has introduced Alethia to one of the most effective ways of handling resentments. By using this technique, she breaks the resentment cycle and mentally shifts gears. The chain of negative thoughts is deliberately broken by injecting some positive ideas. These positive ideas are incompatible with an anxious state of mind and serve to extinguish the undesirable response.

RESENTMENT TEST

Here is a test to help you decide the depth of your resentment and whether you really want to do something about it. Write down your resentment. Then read the questions. Check each statement as to how it applies to your feeling about your resentment. Check it true or false by circling T or F. After completing the test, follow the instructions below.

RESENTMENT _____

1. T (F) I like living in the past rather than the present.
2. (T) F I prefer to live in the present rather than in the past.
3. T (F) I want my resentment more than I want my freedom.
4. (T) F I want to be free from emotional bondage.
5. T (F) I enjoy looking backward to the things that have hurt me.
6. (T) F I prefer to look ahead at good things rather than back to bad things.
7. T (F) I enjoy having a wall between me and the person who has hurt me.
8. (T) F I want to break down the barriers that separate me from my spouse or children.
9. T (F) I like the role of being the reactor to the way another person behaves.
10. (T) F I want to be a proactor and take the initiative in life.
11. T (F) I get great satisfaction in "getting even" with my spouse.
12. (T) F I want to be free from thoughts of revenge.
13. T (F) I enjoy suffering as a martyr.
14. T (F) I want to be free from the need to be a martyr.

Add the number of trues for both the even and the odd numbers.
    Odd Numbers ___0___ Even Numbers __6__
Take the even number scores.
    1-4   First-class resenter.
    5-10 On the right track, but still a good way to go.
    10-14 Go to it and do something about it.

The Decisive Motivational Action

Here is a plan of action for you to use in handling your resentments. You'll have to take them one at a time.

1. Pinpoint your problem. State it in behavioral terms, "I keep thinking about Ed losing our money at Las Vegas."
2. Make a Xerox copy of the card below.
3. Think about the person whom you resent and as objectively as possible, write down six good points about him or her.
4. Keep this card in your pocketbook or billfold.
5. When you begin to think negative thoughts about this person, go into action.
   a. Remove the card and look at it.
   b. Concentrate on STOP. Say it out LOUD. If convenient, SHOUT!
   c. Read and concentrate on the six good points about the person whom you resent.

RESENTMENT REDUCER

PROBLEM _____

STOP

The moment the cue comes—go into ACTION
  *Concentrate on **STOP.**
    *Say it out **LOUD.**
      *If convenient, **SHOUT!**

THINK

Six of resentee's good points:

_____
_____
_____
_____
_____
_____

Action Strategy #6

TRADE BEHAVIORS WITH YOUR PARTNER

Dr. Paul Popenoe used to say that Americans claimed to be monogamous but actually practiced a form of polygamy. Unlike the admittedly polygamous peoples, many Americans have more than one wife, but not all at once. They take them one at a time. This process is referred to as "serial polygamy."

There are various ways of accomplishing this including the relatively new practice of trading. What is called "The Most Unique Trade in Baseball History" took place in 1973. It involved two women, wives of pitchers on a professional baseball team. Because of the incident, the husbands came to be known as "switch pitchers." The two husbands and wives, who had been a happy, close foursome for a long time, decided to trade partners. The whole thing was carefully arranged with the older child of each marriage living with his father and the younger one with his mother. They even agreed to trade the family dogs.

At last report—the whole deal had gone sour. The problem might have been that they had traded the wrong things.

If you are dissatisfied with your spouse, a trade might be a good idea, but instead of trading your spouse, trade behaviors.

The Way Warren & Brenda Morgan Did It

Warren and Brenda Morgan both claimed they had a good marriage but there were some uneasy moments in their relationship. These were dismissed as "the trivial little troubles that everybody has."

Brenda had grown up in a home where her father had always indulged his daughter. Consequently, she had never developed a sense of punctuality. It became a family joke that Brenda would be late for her own funeral. She *was* late, an hour no less, for her wedding. Warren was irritated, but he reasoned it was a bride's privilege.

As the problem grew, so did his frustration. It seemed that Brenda was never on time. On the rare occasions when she was dressed before her husband, she would immediately start to do some household chore while there was a spare moment. Warren confided to his friend Joe, "Just once I would like to see Brenda waiting in the car for me the way I always have to for her."

Many of Brenda's foibles that had intrigued and amused him in dating days grew to be thoroughly maddening. After a few years he began to verbalize these criticisms. Unfortunately, he did not always choose the best time for his comments. Though Brenda forced a smile, she was furious when he made these statements in the company of her friends.

Brenda wasn't about to take it lying down. She responded with spirit and it wasn't long before the sparks were really flying. And Brenda was no mean contender when it came to verbal skills. This became another thorn in Warren's side. When they were in the company of others, she was the star performer. If Warren began to tell a cherished fish story, he would hardly get underway before Brenda jumped in and took over the conversation. Increasingly, Warren had the feeling that he had never been able to finish a conversation.

During his college career, Warren had taken some psychology courses which caused him to wonder if Brenda sublimated her sex drive through her constant talking. But Brenda saw it another way. She was an affectionate person who wanted love, "not just sex." After a snide remark by a frustrated Warren she replied, "I certainly like to *make love* but love and sex can easily be two different things. The only time you ever kiss me is when you want sex. And I can't remember when you last told me you loved me."

Perhaps it was this sense of frustration that caused Brenda to overindulge the children. The children had quickly caught on and soon had her wound around their tiny fingers. Warren had cheerfully gone along with this at first, but he became increasingly critical of what he considered excessive expenditures on the children.

On one occasion when he was complaining about the amount of money they had been spending on children's clothing, Brenda turned on him "What do *you* know about clothes? I spend more time picking up after you than I do the children." This became a point of conflict between them. Warren's mother had always uncomplainingly picked up after her son and he had grown up believing this was a woman's duty.

After an encounter in which both said many more things than they intended, they decided to seek some help and made an appointment to see a counselor. Both of them felt rather apprehensive about the initial interview, but the counselor proved to be very understanding. He also explained to them that he didn't intend to spend too much time examining the past but would focus on present behavior. The counselor provided them with paper and pencil so that they could work their way through a series of steps.

STEP ONE: Learning To Communicate Verbally

Warren and Brenda were led to see that any trade is preceded by a period of bargaining. If exchanging behaviors is to be effective, there must be communication between the two partners involved.

They discovered communication is always taking place between two people. Even when they are not talking, they may still be communicating. In fact, silence is one of the most effective ways of conveying hostility.

Warren and Brenda came to understand that, before any changes could take place, they must learn how to communicate *verbally*—putting the issues into words.

They set a specific time when the relationship would be discussed—Thursday night at 7:00 P.M.

When the time arrived, they set up ground rules. They agreed there would be:

1. No attempts to go back over past history. All discussion would be about the present.
2. No "zaps." Zaps are insulting statements that husbands and wives make to each other. As they are discussing what to do about getting Jimmy to Little League, Brenda insists that Warren take his turn, whereupon he responds, "You certainly are a nagger." Brenda warns, "That's a zap," and Warren apologizes.

3. No blaming. The counselor led Brenda and Warren to see that a married person has a built-in alibi. When anything goes wrong, he or she can blame his or her spouse. This alibi must be eliminated so the basic principle is to insist that neither spouse is to attempt to blame the other for the situation. Each agrees to focus on his or her own behavior in the relationship.

4. No threats or ultimatums.

With these ground rules laid, Brenda and Warren are now ready to enter into an adult discussion of the situation and the further steps that need to be taken.

STEP TWO: Pinpoint The Undesirable Behaviors of Your Spouse

If there is going to be a successful trading of behaviors, it is important to pinpoint the troubled areas. Statements such as: "She is just too immature"; "He's a big put-on"; "That was a cop-out" are too vague. The statements need to be much more specific.

Using the forms the counselor had provided, Warren and Brenda both sat down to think out their situation and try to pinpoint the exact areas of aggravation. They were asked to list these in order, choosing three—with number one as the most sensitive issue; number two, not so sensitive; and number three, least sensitive.

They discovered the process wasn't nearly as easy as they had at first imagined. Brenda, who had been so certain at the beginning, had to do some careful considering before she finally came up with her list which read:

1. He only tells me he loves me when we are having sex.
2. He criticizes me in front of other people.
3. He drops his clothes all over the place.

Warren spent a lot of time working on his list and, like Brenda, he discovered pinpointing to be a difficult process.

1. She fails to discipline the children.
2. She interrupts me when I'm speaking.
3. She is always late.

At last they have it out in the open. Previously, they had thought dark thoughts about each other and occasionally uttered veiled protests. Now, these have become specific and precise. However, the situation is still fluid and these conclusions are open for reconsideration and may be amended later.

STEP THREE: Label Your Responses to Your Spouse's Actions

They now believed that all behavior is carried on for the rewards it brings to the person involved and that husband and wife interact with each other. It was also important for Warren and Brenda to discover what the other person's behavior was doing to or for each of them so they could once again pinpoint individual reactions.

Warren notes his reactions to Brenda's behaviors:

1. When I watch the children dominating our home, I feel as if I don't really count. I'm just the meal ticket to provide the money for financing the family.
2. When she interrupts, I feel as if she is downgrading me in front of our friends.
3. This constant lateness reinforces the feeling that what I want to do is of no importance. I might as well not be on time myself.

Brenda reacts to Warren's behaviors:

1. His lack of affection turns me off sexually. I don't want him to touch me.
2. When he criticizes me in front of others, I feel he's cutting me down to size.
3. Picking up clothes is such a simple thing. It almost seems as if he is purposely irritating me by leaving them lying around.

An examination of these reactions shows the manner in which their reactions support each other's behavior. Now that they have some insight into these supporting behaviors, they are ready to go to work on doing something about the behaviors they find so objectionable.

STEP FOUR: State The Desirable Positive Behaviors of a Spouse

If Warren and Brenda spend all their time thinking up undesirable behaviors they see in each other, they may develop a critical, negative attitude. It is important that they consider some good things about their marriage. When they do so, they each find something of value about their relationship and each proceeds to indicate it to the other.

When Warren comes to Brenda's good points, he can see many that are immediately obvious.

1. Brenda has a sweet outgoing personality.
2. Brenda keeps the house neat and tidy.
3. Brenda dresses well so that I am proud to introduce her as my wife.

In this part of the plan of action, they have both taken a major step in stating their spouse's areas of strength.

Brenda goes to work on her list of desirable positive behaviors of Warren and comes up with the following list:

1. He earns a good living; makes better wages than most men.
2. He takes an interest in civic affairs, belongs to the Civitans, and attends P.T.A.
3. He does chores like looking after the yard.

After they have written these in rough form, the counselor suggests they rewrite the behaviors on what he calls a Pinpoint Worksheet. They both note the change in sequence. Desirable positive behaviors are listed first. The revised worksheet is as follows:

BRENDA'S PINPOINTING WORKSHEET

I. *Desirable or positive behaviors of spouse.*
   1. *He earns a good living, makes better wages than most men.*
   2. *He takes an interest in civic affairs, belongs to the Civitans, and attends P.T.A.*
   3. *Does chores like looking after the yard.*
II. *Undesirable behaviors of spouse.*
   1. *He only tells me he loves me when we are having sex.*
   2. *He criticizes me in front of other people.*
   3. *He drops his clothes all over the place.*
III. *My reactions to these behaviors.*
   1. *His lack of affection turns me off-sexually. I don't want him to touch me.*
   2. *When he criticizes me in front of others I feel he's cutting me down to size.*
   3. *Picking up clothes is such a simple thing. It almost seems as if he is purposely irritating me by leaving them lying around.*

WARREN'S PINPOINTING WORKSHEET

I. *Desirable or positive behaviors of spouse.*
   1. *Brenda has a sweet outgoing personality.*
   2. *Brenda keeps the house neat and tidy.*
   3. *Brenda dresses well so that I am proud to introduce her as my wife.*
II. *Undesirable behaviors of spouse.*
   1. *She fails to discipline the children.*
   2. *She interrupts me when I'm speaking.*
   3. *She is always late.*
III. *My reactions to these behaviors.*
   1. *When I watch the children dominating our home I feel as if I don't really count. I'm just the meal ticket to provide for financing the family.*
   2. *When she interrupts I feel as if she is downgrading me in front of our friends.*
   3. *This constant lateness reinforces the feeling that what I want to do is of no importance. I might as well not be on time.*

STEP FIVE: Negotiating a Contract

Warren and Brenda are guided to take the least volatile of the behaviors and decide what they will contract to do. The two obvious behaviors are Warren's untidiness and Brenda's lateness. They make a contract which will call for Brenda to be on time and Warren to develop some tidy habits.

WARREN AND BRENDA'S BEHAVIORAL-EXCHANGE CONTRACT #1

Warren agrees he will keep the bedroom tidy and pick up his clothes. Brenda in turn agrees she will be on time for whatever events they attend together.

STEP SIX: Counting The Behaviors

For one week Warren and Brenda go about implementing their behavioral exchange contract. They use a graph to record their performance during that week. They prepare a chart which is placed in a prominent place such as the refrigerator or the bathroom mirror. Warren scores the number of times Brenda was on time and Brenda records the times Warren left the bedroom tidy.

BEHAVIORAL-EXCHANGE
CONTRACT #1

TARGET BEHAVIORS: * Brenda will be on time for whatever events they attend togehter.
* Warren will keep the bedroom tidy and pick up his clothes.

OBSERVERS: Warren to observe Brenda and Brenda to observe Warren.

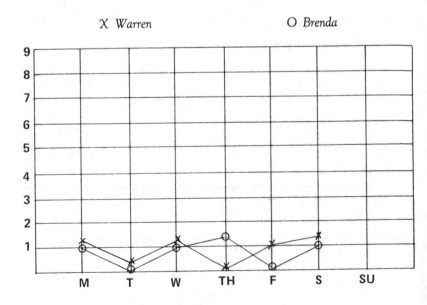

X Warren   O Brenda

STEP SEVEN: Renegotiating The Contract

After the first week Warren and Brenda sat down to check on their progress. Warren's behavior was fairly simple to assess as the room could be checked each day. Estimating Brenda's punctuality wasn't quite so easy. They had to agree in advance on what time they would leave. Then they were able to determine whether she had been ready at that time. The most important result was that they both became aware of these behaviors.

They had to make a decision. Should they continue to focus on these behaviors for another week or would they move on?

When they felt ready, they moved to the next behavior.

Of all the presidents, few have captured the imagination of Americans as did Theodore Roosevelt. The supreme actionist, he propelled himself into an infinite variety of activities. A relative once remarked, "Theodore wanted to be the groom at every wedding and the corpse at every funeral." Supremely, he was the man of strengths, speaking softly while wielding a big stick.

But that wasn't the way it all began. Young Theodore had trouble with his eyes and a weak body wracked with periodic asthmatic attacks. An aunt compared him to a "pale azalea." When he was eleven years old, his father told him, "You have the mind but not the body." To which the indomitable Teddy replied, "I'll *make* my body." And make it he did.

You must *make* your marriage. It's not going to happen automatically. By scientifically using the principles of behavior outlined in this chapter you can build a strong, workable relationship.

Action Strategy #7

GET OFF THE EMOTIONAL ROLLER COASTER

"You don't do what you do because you feel the way you feel—you feel the way you feel because you do what you do—In other words, your actions will determine how you feel."[1]

Love, courtship, and marriage are highly charged with emotion. The experience of falling in love is often inexplicable, exhilarating, devastating. The dating game is full of excitement and danger and possibly some overtones of guilt. Marriage is entered upon with high anticipation—the thrill of being center stage in the wedding ceremony, a rapturous honeymoon. The birth of the first child brings all the fluctuations of joy, dread, and sometimes downright fear. Thus goes the pattern of life—night and day, delight and despair, sunlight and shadows.

With all of the highs and lows of living, the husband and wife may feel emotionally drained and depressed. "The joy is gone." "I don't feel right about it." "I'm not happy." In a final ironic twist, divorce may be considered the one last resort for finding true happiness. And the most depressing day of all may be that on which the divorce decree becomes absolute.

Feeling has become so important in our day that a widespread philosophy maintains, "Man is what he feels." This emphasis has led us down some strange pathways. We have become a nation of emotional indulgers. We cry over soap operas. We pay good money to watch horror movies that scare the daylights out of us. We yell for joy while men batter each other to a bloody pulp in the ring. We pop pills and guzzle liquor. And we let it all hang out in so-called "sensitivity" groups that may be the most insolent attack ever launched on people's finer feelings.

Of course, few of us would want a dull, drab, gray, monotonous life without feelings—no highs or lows, ups or downs. So much do we come to value these emotional experiences that we will pay any price to acquire them. At its worst, the search for highs and lows leads to drugs—uppers and downers and alcohol. At its best, the quest for excitement leads to ventures launched by intrepid thrill-seekers which, by a strange turn of the wheel, may ultimately prove to benefit mankind.

Within the inner sanctums of our personality, emotional reactions reveal some of our most vulnerable areas. We greet each other on this level. "How are you feeling?" "I feel like a million dollars!" "I feel awful." In their milder manifestations, these feelings include elation, excitement, anxieties, fears, and apprehensions. In their more serious forms, we plummet to the dark depths of depression, rise with the unbridled elation of mania, or suffer the pendulum swing of manic-depressive psychosis.

Confronted with these shattering emotions, the subject has to decide the best way to cope. There are a number of alternative strategies, some of which are not without their pitfalls.

The Chemical Approach

Body chemistry has always held a fascination for medical

research. As the search proceeded with considerable success, there was always the hope that in the same way that a chemical could heal the body, there might be chemicals that would heal the emotional problems that beset the human mind. There were periodic breakthroughs. One of these moments came with the realization of the potency of the tranquilizer. This family of drugs quickly gained wide popularity. Soon tranquilizers were being used to treat everything from alcohol withdrawal and epileptic seizures to divorce anxiety. One of these drugs, Valium, is now the most widely prescribed drug in America.

The drug companies, having invested so much time and money in research and development, have launched tremendous advertising campaigns among medical doctors to promote their sales. One widely distributed journal of the prestigious American Psychiatric Association produced a recent issue containing twenty pages of advertising. Of these, sixteen pages, including front and back covers, were used to advertise drugs for the "mentally ill." They were advertised as being appropriate for "controlling anxiety, tension and agitation," "anti-depressant," "helps weather the manic storm," "provides effective control of psychotic symptoms," "stops the crisis." A layman reading such a magazine is likely to conclude that the use of drugs is the only way to deal with emotional problems.

This tendency to see drugs as a simple panacea for emotional difficulties has brought with it its own peculiar problems as in the case of Betty Ford, ex-first lady of the United States. Mrs. Ford has been a trailblazer in many ways. She has undergone a widely-publicized mastectomy, acquired a CB radio with the handle of "Big Mama," and shed her wrinkles with a facelift. But her most trying moment came when she openly acknowledged she had become dependent upon drugs and alcohol and admitted herself to a hospital.

The decision to enter the hospital was reached after a traumatic confrontation with her family. She describes her reaction following the family encounter: "At first I was bitter toward the medical profession for all those years I was advised to take pills rather than wait for the pain to hit. I took pills for pain and pills to sleep. Today, many doctors are beginning to recognize the risks in these medications, but some of them are all too eager to write prescriptions."

A doctor who had sat in on the original Ford family confrontation gave Mrs. Ford the volume, *Alcoholics Anonymous*, with some specific directions. She said, "He told me to read the book, substituting the words *chemically dependent* for *alcoholic*. Since a tranquilizer or dry martini brings the same relief, you can use the same book for drugs and alcohol. And when I say drugs, I'm talking about legal medications prescribed by doctors." Later Mrs. Ford was able to acknowledge the use of another drug—alcohol. She issued a statement, "I have found that I am not only addicted to the medication I have been taking for my arthritis but also to alcohol."[2] The major trouble was that all these drugs, including alcohol, were all perfectly legitimate but were just as dangerous and led to a dead-end street.

Drug therapy for emotional disturbances has not been satisfactory. At best, drugs are a crutch to help the sufferer over a tough spot. Once the crutch becomes a necessary part of everyday living, it can easily become a tyrannical monster. One of the biggest problems is that many people are frightened to give up their drugs! The chemical approach is imprecise and inexact and may easily cause more problems than it solves.

The Catharsis Premise

All of this has led to a new formula for handling the

problems of life by a technique referred to variously as ventilation, abreaction, catharsis. One author claims that "... the expression of anger is a healthy thing," and that people adept in assertiveness training can "express anger in nondestructive ways." This *seems* to indicate that anger must be expressed, and if it isn't ventilated there is danger of a destructive manifestation in such forms as migraine headaches, asthma, ulcers, and skin problems.

David Norman is annoyed with Monica, his wife, who has finally admitted overspending the budget for some cute little dresses on sale at Neiman-Marcus.

"But, honey, can't you see I saved fifty dollars by buying while they were on sale?"

"Saved fifty dollars! I am sick to death of spending money to save money!"

"Do you want your wife to go around wearing old clothes?"

"My dear, you've got more clothes than any other three women. There are dresses in your closet that you've never worn twice."

"I'm surprised at you, David, but I should have known. You always have been a tightwad."

"What do you mean—a tightwad?"

So the exchange grows more heated as David and Monica enter into a verbal slugfest.

The following evening they have a long talk, and Monica snuggles up to David, "I'm so glad I took those psychology courses. Isn't it good the way we can express ourselves and drain off our emotions? Our quarrel has been a therapeutic experience."

Norman, still smarting from the sting of Monica's tart tongue, wonders about that.

The validity of Monica's idea that expression of emotion helps to drain them has both proponents and opponents.

There are some good reasons to doubt this premise.

From observation, it seems that constant expression of emotions not only does *not* drain the emotions but may reinforce these reactions. If action brings on feeling, this may simply bring on a more intensive feeling.

Take the case of Charla and Jack Donovan. Jack has a hair-trigger temper, and this in turn sparks anger in Charla. Charla says, "He gets mad and flies off the handle at me. I can stand it for a while, then I have to strike back at him. Sometimes we stay mad at each other for several days. And it usually starts over a triviality."

This is the tragedy of people who believe in expressing their emotions. A family is an interacting unit. In the process of expressing emotions, the people who get hurt are the ones we love most of all.

Albert Bandura's study of aggression has raised many questions about the validity of the catharsis hypothesis. Children who were permitted to practice aggressive behavior in the hope that the activity might be reduced have maintained the behavior at the same level or actually increased its frequency. Similarly, with adults given opportunities to shock other people under non-retaliative conditions: the more aggressive the behaviors, the more punitive they became. Other studies indicate people who air their hostility often became increasingly hostile.[3]

Angry outbursts can have several bad effects. The subject learns and practices the wrong skill. The child, given to fits of rage, early learns to "control by tantrum." As these expressions bring responses of awe and submission from others, he is reinforced in his outbursts and continues to use them as a means of control. Thus, he has learned a self-perpetuating behavior. He also successfully alienates others so that he comes to live an increasingly isolated existence. Other people, particularly members of his family, learn to avoid him. The subject lives in a state of turmoil which takes its toll on his own health.

As for the claims that fighting between husband and wife is a healthy activity, I must confess I have grave doubts. Primitive man lived a precarious existence. If he were to survive, he could use one of two mechanisms—fight or flight. In his modern setting, twentieth-century man is frequently faced with more subtle threats—not so much to his existence, but to his status. These threats come from the most unexpected quarters, including his marriage.

As a marriage relationship deteriorates, the experience within which two people should be fundamentally concerned about each other can become irritating and thoroughly annoying to each of the participants. In this situation the fight or flight mechanism emerges and often becomes the fight *and* flight reaction. Fighting and bickering lead to life lived at such a level of tension that flight seems to offer the only solution. Eventually one or both flee to the divorce court for refuge.

"Man is what he feels" has ushered in a reign of terror. Resentful people, as we have already noted, may be completely immobilized by emotional reactions from some event that took place in the distant past and is keeping them in subjection. They are prisoners of the past. The Decisive Motivational Action concept rejects this idea and provides another alternative.

Another Way

"I want to apologize . . ." The speaker is standing before a group of residents in the "house," a self-help community for drug addicts. The downstairs room in which they are gathered is typical of the rather frowzy, two-story frame building which has seen better days.

The young man has been in trouble, and his fellow

house members have administered discipline by demoting him to one of the low-status positions in the life of the community. On this particular morning he says penitently, "I want to apologize to the house. I have been indulging—and I commit myself to stop it."

What was this man indulging in—drugs, food, stealing money? No, none of these. He has been glum, gloomy, and depressed. Instead of saying he has been depressed as if he were the victim of some impersonal force, he says he is "indulging." He admits responsibility for his depression.

Abraham Lincoln, who put so many great truths into homely and easily understood language, said, "Many people are about as happy as they choose to be." The theme has been taken up by two Christian psychiatrists who set forth their basic concept in the words: "Happiness is a choice." This element of choice is frequently overlooked. Instead of being overwhelmed by our emotions, we must utilize the Decisive Motivational Action.

William James, the great pioneer in the psychology of religion, spoke significantly about the Action Principle. He may have given us a clue to understanding how we are responsible for our feelings by theorizing that action might precede emotional reaction. "There is, accordingly, no better known or more generally useful precept in the moral training of youth, or in one's personal self-discipline, than that which bids us pay primary attention to what we do and express, and not care too much for what we feel . . . Action seems to follow feelings, but really action and feeling go together; and by regulating the action, which is under the more direct control of the will we can indirectly regulate the feeling, which is not."

At least partial confirmation of this approach comes from those highly effective small groups sometimes referred to as the peer group psychotherapy groups. One of these groups stated, "We can't stop feeling, but we can direct behavior." Here is the frank acknowledgment of impotence in the area of emotions. Through the most powerful force known to behavioral scientists, "peer group pressures," people can be made to change their behavior.

The second self-help statement further emphasizes the Decisive Motivational Action: "Do the thing, and the rewards will emerge." This change in behavior may be the key to handling an emotional problem through the strategy of managing behavior. An individual's emotional reactions are complex, but an action program can put them under control. This opens the door to all sorts of possibilities as to what may be accomplished by the Decisive Motivational Action.

Though it is difficult to produce hard evidence, some investigators are picking up on the old idea that the emotional states may be associated with chemical changes in the body and that these chemical levels are related to the body's activity. A professor of physical education has reported what he calls a "significant relationship" between changes in certain hormone levels in executives brought on by exercise and their emotional stability. A psychiatrist has joined the physiologist in advancing the action-leading-to-chemical-change theory, seeing the brain as being subject to this change. He is presently working with researchers at the National Institute of Mental Health inquiring into the possibilities of this theory.

The effects of exercise on mental health have been so positive that eager investigators are making enthusiastic claims. A psychiatrist has stated his conviction that mild depression is more common than the common cold but can be markedly helped by slow endurance exercise. A writer, in a burst of euphoria, has proclaimed that weekend jogging activities "could well be the basis for the nation's first grass-roots movement in community mental health."

Even more conventional psychotherapists, seeking to discover the content of the unconscious, are now claiming that people who participate in marathon runs from fourteen to eighteen miles in duration will complete their effort in a condition that makes them ideal subjects for psychotherapy. Running seems to break down psychological barriers, and the runners can verbalize childhood memories or problems. For these therapists, it seems exercise has opened a channel to the unconscious. Some of them have been willing to admit exercise is just as effective as the traditional "talk-cure" techniques.

Some mental health professionals have apparently just run upon (in more ways than one) the idea of exercise helping with emotional problems. One psychiatrist who had taken up jogging with the hope of building his own physical fitness suddenly discovered the activity might have another application. Looking at his fellow joggers, he concluded, "Nobody jogging down the track appears to be depressed." Noting that 70 percent of his patients were depressives, he quickly added exercise to his list of treatments and concluded that exercise is more effective than pills in controlling depression. He discovered that 15 percent to 20 percent depressives shared a quick benefit after as little as a week of running.

Handling a Grief Reaction

Grief is possibly the most emotionally devastating of all the experiences that beset the human spirit. It can take many forms—death of a family member, separation from a loved one, a divorce. Handling the grief reaction has proved difficult and often leaves the sufferer living in a strange, isolated world from which it seems there is no escape. One widower in a meeting of singles, most of whom were divorced people, turned on them, "I don't really belong here. Most of you wanted to get rid of your spouse and worked toward separation from your partner. I loved my wife and she loved me. She didn't want to leave me and I certainly didn't want her to go. It's not fair." The group sat shocked at the unfairness of his implications. Yet, they knew he was going through a grief experience, a variety of which they had already experienced.

A woman who had lost her husband by death had written the story of her experience. The book was successful and had brought grief-stricken people to her door for counseling. With a sense of hypocrisy, she began to slip back into the hazy world of depression. Nightmares beset her and she resorted to her tranquilizers. While in a stupor, she fell in what could have been a dangerous accident. Yet, it helped to bring her to her senses.

Then she recalled a memory of her girlhood days. When she had been upset, frustrated, or annoyed she would rush out, jump on her bike, and ride for hours. With the wind cooling her face, she would ride and ride until her hurt or anger had disappeared. Why not try the bike again?

She started with a stationary bike. When she awakened in the night and looked at the dreaded, surrounding blackness, she forced herself to climb out of bed onto the bicycle and peddled until she felt better. Then she invested in a ten-speed bike and went riding in the park. At first it was all weak knees and sore muscles. With the passing of time she had a growing consciousness of ". . . what a marvelous tranquilizer exercise is." It began to show. Thighs firmed up. Hips trimmed down. She bought some new clothes to acknowledge her growing sense of self-value.

The grieving widow's testimony became clear and specific: "Bicycling has made me aware that my body is important and should be treated well, not just taken for granted. I discovered my body could help me relax, even stop worrying if I used it correctly. The exercise I was getting made an almost magical change in my disposition and outlook. I was calmer, enjoyed life more, slept better." This widow had discovered the importance of action in helping her through the most devastating of all emotional experiences—the loss of a loved one.

As a young and inexperienced pastor I was vividly aware of my inadequacy in trying to minister to a family who had lost the mother who had worked for years to raise her family of four. The daughters sat around weeping. I tried to ask some appropriate questions which were answered in indiscernable monosyllables. Then Chap arrived. A favorite son-in-law of the deceased lady, he sized up the situation in a moment and moved into action. "Okay, girls, let's get going. The dishes need doing, the carpet sweeping, and there are clothes to be washed. Mother wouldn't want us to be sitting around weeping." While I, the spiritual guide and mentor, sat helplessly by, this bright layman had spurred the whole group into action.

It has long been known that grief involves pain and a period of time in which this pain is "worked through." The "working-through" process is frequently referred to as "grief work." Acting—doing something—is clearly a significant but frequently overlooked part of handling the painful aftermath of traumatic separation experiences.

The Neglected Factor of Restitution

Look who's teaching the Bible! In a burgeoning interest in Bible study, a wide variety of groups have sprung up in the most unlikely places. There are Bible clubs in schools, study groups in offices, and home Bible groups where housewives diligently pore over this fascinating book. Perhaps most surprising of all, alcoholics are teaching some of the most neglected truths of the Bible. Preeminent among these is the idea of restitution.

Alcoholics Anonymous, the most successful organization in rehabilitating the alcoholic, owes much of its success to the remarkable set of behavioral principles known as "The Twelve Steps." Steps eight and nine are especially significant:

8. Made a list of all the people we had harmed and became willing to make amends to them.
9. Made direct amends to such people whenever possible.[4]

Strange though it may seem, this secular organization is recalling us to the biblical idea of restitution or "putting back."

There is a judge within us who demands restitution. His name is conscience. When an individual has violated his or her values, the internal value system demands action. The most common manifestation of guilt is anxiety or depression. Feelings of low self-worth and apprehension may, in actual fact, be a form of self-punishment. The way to handle them could be to undertake some act of restitution.

People who have been emotionally overwhelmed often describe themselves as "weak," "tired," "no energy." Because of this feeling, they generally take to the bed to "rest up" and "regain their energies." Many a doctor has aided and abetted the situation by telling his anxious patient to "take it easy" for a few days. Some research has shown this may be exactly opposite of what these people should do. They really need purposeful action. Action which leads to involvement (assisting someone else in need of help) is the most rewarding of all.

John Donne stated it beautifully:

> No man is an island, entire of itself;
> every man is a piece of the continent, a part
> of the main;
> if a clod be washed away by the sea, Europe
> is the less, as well as if a promontory were,
> as well as if a manor of thy friends, or of
> thine own were; any man's death diminishes me,
> because I am involved in Mankind;
> and therefore never send to know for whom the
> bell tolls; it tolls for thee.

The Decisive Motivational Action

Are your emotional reactions dominating you? Why not get them under control? Here is a plan of action.

1. Recall past anxiety experiences—the way in which anxiety and depression rolled over you and left you feeling hopeless and helpless.

2. Make a resolution that you are going to break the tyranny of emotions. Despite the pain, you did get a certain satisfaction from your emotional debauch. Decide to relinquish these satisfactions so you can get control of your life.

3. Face the fact that tranquilizers and other pills are, at best, a crutch to get you over a tough spot. Beware of becoming a pill popper.

4. Remember the actions that might have led you into this situation. If you have violated your value system, guilt may be bothering you.

5. Perhaps you need to confess a problem between you and another person. It will probably help you to get it out in the open.

6. It is easy to confuse depression with physical weakness and to feel the need for bed rest. This generally doesn't help. Don't spend your time lying around. Get into action.

7. There may be some act of restitution you need to undertake. Has your behavior hurt someone? Remember the AA Plan: "Made a list of the people we had harmed and became willing to make amends to them. Made direct amends to such people whenever possible."

8. Recall the statements: "As our behaviors go, so go our feelings or emotions."[5] (Diebert and Harmon) "It is much easier to act yourself into a new way of feeling than to feel yourself into a new way of acting." (E. Stanley Jones)

9. Undertake some plan of action. Get moving. ACT. ACT. ACT.

Action Strategy #8

ACT "AS IF"

"If you want a quality, act as if you already had it."
WILLIAM JAMES

Movie actor Jay Robinson created a name for himself in his role as the Emperor Caligula in the movie, "The Robe." His acting attracted a lot of attention and, when he signed a contract with 20th Century Fox, it seemed as if he were headed toward a notable career. But his success was short-lived, and he was released from his contract. In reaction to his misfortune, he sought consolation in drugs. Following an arrest on a narcotics charge, he spent seventeen months in a California prison.

After his release from prison, Robinson set about to rebuild his career. He accepted a role in the movie, "Born Again," the story of Chuck Colson of Nixon White House fame. While acting in the movie, he came in contact with Dean Jones, a dedicated Christian who played the lead role. Through Jones' witness, Robinson became a believer. Acting a certain type of role led him into a whole new way of life.

Drama and human personality have had some interesting parallels. The Grecian actor on stage in the amphitheater wore a mask on his face. The word *mask* came to be associated with the word *personality*. The relationship of acting and personality has been reinforced by Shakespeare's famous lines: "All the world's a stage, and all the men and women merely players: they have their exits and their entrances; and one man in his time plays many parts, his acts being seven ages." This statement suggests that the levels of maturation through which we must all inevitably pass in our growth and development are acted out on the stage of life.

But there is a more potent linking of acting and personality in the "act-as-if" concept. No special dramatic ability is required. Each of us has the potentiality for self-change if we learn to "act as if."

Basic to our idea of the action premise is the notion that actions taken in different areas can bring beneficial results. We must assume people can change. Unfortunately, husbands and wives often fall into the trap that human nature is fixed and unchangeable; therefore, any hope for change is futile.

> "That's the way he is."
> "Her mother was the same way. She'll never change."
> "I know exactly what he'll do."

The action premise brings another perspective. It says we *can* learn new skills. We are not limited by our past experiences.

The soap opera has become the epitome of unreality, fantasy, and escapism for many Americans. Yet, some facets of it may have something to teach us. A recent writer on the "soaps" claims that actors shape their parts or are shaped by them. The role of one chubby actress called for her to play the part of an unhappy, fat girl who decided to go on a diet. The actress got so carried away with her role that she kept on dieting and lost fifty-seven pounds! By "acting as if," she had learned to diet.

"Acting as if" is the pathway taken by many great innovators of mankind. By using this technique, they have made revolutionary discoveries for the betterment of their fellows. Semmelweis, a Hungarian obstetrician who lived in the early nineteenth century, was concerned with the number of women in one hospital area dying of childbirth fever. Patients in a companion clinic at the same hospital had a much lower mortality rate.

Observing carefully, he noted that the students who examined the women in the high mortality ward came directly from the dissecting room. He decided he was going to "act as if" the students in the high mortality clinic were carrying disease on unwashed hands and gave the startling direction that they should all wash their hands before examining patients. By "acting as if," Semmelweis solved a critical medical problem with lasting benefits.

A similar situation exists in marriage today. Few marriages are anywhere near what they could be. Most husbands and wives have shown an amazing lack of imagination in utilizing the potentialities that exist in their relationship. There are a jillion things that could be done to improve our lives together, but we fail to do anything about these possibilities.

A television program on Knute Rockne, the celebrated coach of Notre Dame, told of Rockne's ability, not only to affect his team, but also to affect himself with the "act-as-if" formula. The Notre Dame team was losing the game. With halftime in the offing, the coach searched about for some dynamic message to give in the locker room. He was so enthusiastic and convincing that the team members were fired up and there was a dramatic resurgence of spirit.

Inspired, they went back to the playing field to win the game.

That night, traveling back with a friend on the train, they were discussing the dramatic turnaround in the game. Rockne suddenly said, "What's more, I'm going to write those Eastern alumni and demand an apology from them!" In "acting as if" the Eastern alums were against him, he had convinced himself they were.

Living in a skeptical society where the sorry state of marriage is a recurring theme in song, story, and television, the prevailing image is that of flawed marital relationships. "Acting as if" family life were shot, kids a drag, and marriage outmoded, our lives become self-fulfilling prophecies. We must develop a new optimistic outlook on home and family life. One of the ways we are going to be able to do this is by "acting as if."

"Acting as if," we learn new skills. Take Mrs. Simpson—a reluctant parent. She had never been overly enthusiastic about children, but when she became pregnant she was forced to give it a try. However, she didn't do too well. Now, with a boy and girl, she feels completely frustrated.

In her despair, Mrs. Simpson attends a series of sessions for mothers sponsored by the Central Counseling Center. At the third session, she gets her opportunity to talk and makes the most of it. She pours out her hostility and resentment about motherhood: "I never wanted to be a mother. The kids completely frustrate me. I feel as if I'm going to give them the best years of my life and then they'll be up and away." She pauses, looks around and says, "I know I'm not supposed to say this, but I *hate* kids."

The leader of the group gives her the opportunity to get it off her chest. He points out that many people feel the same way. From the book by Becker, *Parents are Teachers*, he reads a statement: "You must take the role of an actor, playing at being a positive parent until you are the parent."[1]

"Take the role of an actor . . ." Kathy Simpson has been introduced to the concept of "act as if." Practitioners using this technique have noticed that affective behavior brings certain satisfactions. Once behavior has been established, it has a momentum of its own.

Deceptive?

The "act-as-if" formula has awesome possibilities for helping troubled marriages. When David McGinnis talked with his counselor about the problem in his marriage, he said, "The difficulty is, there's nothing left in my marriage. I don't love my wife. I used to, but it's all gone now. There's nothing left."

After considerable discussion, the counselor concludes their first session by suggesting some sort of activity. "Why not 'act as if' you love your wife? Give her the same attention you did when you were courting her."

This counsel might not be as trite as it seems. Love is a complex term and involves the three facets of conscious process—knowing, feeling, and willing. The *eros* level of love is emotional; the *philia* level is intellectual; and the *agape* level is volitional or active. When David begins to "act as if" he loves his wife, there is a good chance that the other elements of love might well begin to manifest themselves. There might even be a revival of some of the significant emotional aspects of the love experience.

However, there are a few little problems along the way. David may look at the counselor and say, "I couldn't do that. Don't you guys believe in honesty? I'd be giving a false impression to my wife. It would be deceptive."

David has raised a very interesting point. If he is trying to manipulate his wife so that he can persuade her to do something he wants, then it is deceptive. On the other hand, if he "acts as if" because he wants to learn a new way to accept his responsibilities, he is manipulating himself. As a teaching process, it is good.

"Act as if" to deceive—WRONG!
"Act as if" to learn—GOOD!

Sam Shoemaker put it another way. Questioned as to whether "act as if" were not a hypocritical attitude, he answered that a scientist believes an hypothesis is true for long enough to prove whether it is actually so or not. To take an "act-as-if" stance is to enter an experiment with an open and honest mind. Shoemaker further adds that there is a point when an *experiment* can easily become an *experience.*

The "act-as-if" principle has another significant application. One young man confessed: "For years I tried to find God by reason and logic. I could find no reasons for believing. Then someone told me to "act as if" God existed and see what would happen. I did—and prayer has become a real, life-giving force to me. I live under less pressure, sleep better, make sounder business decisions, give more time to my family, and am generally a much happier, and I hope, more useful member of society." This man made his great spiritual discovery by "acting as if."

Psychosomatic or Somatopsychic?

There was a time when a student of the human species would speak about the physical and emotional aspects of an individual as if these were separate elements. No more.

The great word today among both the physiologists who study the body and psychologists concerned with the mind is *psychosomatic*. This word is made up of two Greek words meaning body and soul and is used to describe the close and intimate relationship between the body and the emotions.

The word *psychosomatic* is generally used to refer to the way the emotions affect the body. Many people sitting in doctor's offices seeking medicine to cure their bodies have nothing at all physically wrong with them. These illnesses are sometimes referred to as "functional" or "psychogenic," implying that the emotions have affected the functioning of the body.

All too little thinking has been given to the reverse situation in the body-emotions relationship. It has been suggested the word *somatopsychic* be used as a means of describing the influence of the body on the emotions. This may then mean that the way we control our bodies affects our emotions and all our feelings toward life. No matter how despondent we may feel, we can "act as if" things were right, conveying this nonverbal message through our body—head held high, smile on our faces, back straight, stomach in, stride forward to meet life. "Act as if" with your body, and your emotional tone will be enhanced.

One of the most frightening things you can ever do is to address a group of your fellow humans. Many a person who can carry on an animated conversation with one or two people, experiences some strange sensations when standing before a group. His tongue thickens. Saliva dries up in his mouth. And the voice he fondly imagined was so rich and resonant proceeds from his lips in a strange, reedy sound.

A man who listened to and criticized over 150,000 speeches in a forty-year period had an answer: "You are afraid to talk because you feel you will fail. You fail because you failed before, so you build a habit of failure." Dale Carnegie suggested that the way to overcome fear of speaking to a group was to gather a number of friends together and begin talking to them. Little by little, confidence will be gained from the success. Carnegie says, "Cure yourself of your fear of speaking by speaking." Of course, he was repeating the old maxim of Emerson who stated the principle in other words: "Do the thing you fear, and the death of fear is certain." By "acting as if," you can change your feelings.

The Decisive Motivational Action

Why not put the "act-as-if" principle to work for you?

1. *How about your work? Dissatisfied? Unhappy? What about a new approach?*

   - *Set off to work enthusiastically. Keep saying, "I'm going to 'act as if' I really like this job."*
   - *When you face a distasteful situation say, "I'm going to 'act as if' I enjoy the challenge of a situation like this."*
   - *What about your attitude toward the boss? Feel he's down on you? Maybe it's **your** attitude. Try "acting as if" you were his favorite. Go ahead and see what a difference it makes.*

2. *What is your relationship with your spouse? Feel as if all the zest has gone out of your relationship? Try an "act as if."*

   - *Hate helping with the housework? "Act as if" you like it. Offer to help with the dishes, clean the rugs. Try to enjoy it.*
   - *Try "acting as if" you and your wife were courting. Surprise her with a box of candy or try bringing home one red rose.*
   - *What is a sport or hobby your husband likes? Football? Fishing? You can't stand it? "Act as if" you like it. You may make some interesting discoveries.*

Action Stragegy #9

MAKE A NEW FRIEND—YOUR SPOUSE

"True friendship is a plant of slow growth."
GEORGE WASHINGTON

Alice and Anton knelt in the front pew of the Hilton Chapel in Chicago. From the brink of the dark valley of psychosis, Anton had written a book titled, *The Exploration of the Inner World*, in which he recounted the story of his emotional pilgrimage. For twenty-seven years he had pursued the woman presently kneeling at his side, and waited for her consent to be his wife. Now after all these years, they were making, of all things, a "covenant of friendship."

Friendship? How quaint this sounds to our sophisticated ears. We find it difficult to comprehend how a man and a woman, both unmarried, would have spent many years in a relationship of friendship. But even more peculiar is the possibility that a husband and wife who have been through the experience of "falling in love" and getting married may refer to each other as "friend."

The feeling of friendship is like that of being comfortably filled with roast beef; love, like the tingle of champagne. While some people may prefer a bubbly drink on occasions (and a goodly proportion of us are not even impressed by bubbly), a continued diet of such a beverage will soon dull the taste buds. The protein-rich beef will have more substance for day in and day out.

If friendship is such a pivotal factor in human relationships, it might be imagined that psychologists, sociologists, and other students of human personality would be devising methods for developing and enhancing this interpersonal skill. But look over the spate of motivational books available today on every conceivable subject. Chances are you'll search in vain for a volume on the "how-to-do-its" of friendship. The closest you may get to such a book is one of the earliest self-help books, *How to Win Friends and Influence People*, by Dale Carnegie.

Where has Friendship Gone?

Whatever happened to friendship? It used to be a much-sought-after human experience. People were willing to spend time and effort in nurturing friendships. But in recent years, the whole idea of friendship has gone into a serious decline. The decline has been so dramatic that we might easily be tempted to conclude there has been a "plot to abolish friendship."

Friendship occupies a unique position among the diversity of human interpersonal encounters. If we charted these relationships, *eros* (romantic) love would stand at one extreme while *agape* (godly) love would be at the opposite pole. The instinctive *eros* is fleshly, rooted in body chemistry and dynamic in its drive. It has a multitude of devotees, ranging all the way from the hardened sensualist to the unsophisticated adolescent. *Agape* love, at the other end of the spectrum, is the highest of all loves, indicating God's initiative in moving toward undeserving men and women.

Between the two extremes—neither altogether selfish nor altruistic; need love nor gift love; human nor divine—stands friendship. It is propagated by neither sensualist nor saint and must be entered upon by voluntary choice. Its writings are so few as to be looked upon in the same way that some people view the pot-bellied stove, streetcar, or poke bonnet!

The psychologists have done little to help our understanding of friendship. For them, the white rat and the pigeon have held an almost fatal fascination. They have been concerned with the types of behavior man shares with the birds and animals. By observing captive rodents running through mazes or pigeons pecking at targets, it is hoped to discover the secrets of human behavior. While there are gregarious animals that seem driven by some inward urge to be with their fellows, animal life knows no equivalent of the shared intellectual apprehension of friendship. Finding no animal counterpart for their laboratory work, experimentally-minded psychologists have virtually ignored friendship as a subject for investigation.

On the other hand, romantic love has had superior public relations channels to assist in its eclipse of friendship. Hollywood portrays the glamor of romance on the screen, to say nothing of the extra-curricular activities of movie actors and actresses. Television dramatizes the agony and ecstasy of female-male encounters suitably dragged out over a series of soap opera episodes. Songwriters churn out the lyrics and hypnotically rhythmic music of romance. Writers toil over reports and exposés and play up the most stimulating aspects of romance—

spewing out a stream of sexually provocative material, sometimes misnamed literature.

Friendship has no special representatives to build its image in a sex-saturated society. When friendship happens to be the theme of a novel or a movie, it is dismissed as quaint, old-fashioned, or Victorian. Nothing gives more evidence of the obsession of our age with *eros* love than the attitude toward friends. Mention that James and Harry are constantly together, and there is a raised eyebrow, knowing smile, and the hint that there are sexual overtones to the relationship.

The Conflict Between Romance and Friendship

Although we have placed friendship on a continuum of human loves, in many ways romance is the antithesis of friendship. The basic differences between these two contending forces are seen in a number of contrasting characteristics.

Romance is fostered by differences. In the throes of infatuation, lovers may confess, "We don't really like each other, but we fell in love." The very differences in background and interests often enhance the romantic episode. When the emotional impact subsides, the lovers may find themselves either antagonists in a protracted conflict or strangers living in two different worlds. Friendship, on the other hand, lacks the emotional sexual reinforcement and depends on a kinship of interests which cement and hold the friends together. The relationship exists because of the *similarity* of background.

Friends and romantic lovers face in different directions. Romantic lovers are face to face. Their preoccupation with each other is so intense that it grows at a very rapid pace until the bubble bursts.

In a conversation with Susan Dowell, I felt as if I were making a visit to a haunted castle with the ghost flitting between us. The "ghost" was Stanley Dane, the young man with whom Susan felt she was "in love." I mentioned the weather and Susan recalled the perfect day when Stanley first held her hand. The discussion of my recent trip to New Mexico caused Susan to remember that if she had not taken her vacation in Florida, she would never have met Stanley. When I mentioned an alumni meeting, Susan launched into a long discourse on Stanley's academic prowess. It mattered not where the conversation started, it all led directly back to Stanley.

Friends take an entirely different posture—side by side, looking in the same direction. Groucho Marx, the acerbic comic, matched wits with guests on his national television program for many years. Few people doubted his intellectual capacity except when it came to selecting a wife. The participant in three unsuccessful marriages, he was attracted to beautiful girls. All his wives were pretty. Asked whether a husband and wife should have similar intellectual levels and interests, he responded, "I could love a stupid woman, but I wouldn't like her. I married my wives because they were pretty and that's not enough reason to marry a woman. You can be fooled by looks. It's better to choose brains." He had discovered that a husband and wife need a shared intellectual outlook.

Romantic lovers tend to idealize the love object and overlook the faults. The young lady involved in a premarital counseling session described her boyfriend as "all that I ever hoped a man might be." When she returned some two years later, she had a somewhat different evaluation of him. She might have profited from the advice of Benjamin Franklin, "Keep your eyes wide open before marriage and half closed after marriage."

Friends accept shortcomings as an integral part of personality.
Benjamin Disraeli, the Prime Minister who led England to
the hour of its greatest glory, was married to the widow of
a former colleague, Mary Anne Wyndham Lewis. As they
entered marriage, Mary Anne compiled what looks
remarkably like a modern personality inventory.

Benjamin	**Mary Anne**
Manners grave and almost sad.	Gay and happy-looking when speaking.
Bad-humored.	Good-humored.
Often says what he does not think.	Never says anything she does not think.
It is impossible to find out whom he likes or dislikes from his manner.	Her manner is quite different, and to those she likes she shows her feelings.
Conceited.	No conceit.
He is seldom amused.	Everything amuses her.
His whole soul is devoted to politics and ambition.	She has no ambition and hates politics.

This willingness to acknowledge and accept her husband's shortcomings may have been an important factor
in the friendship that became the basis for one of the most
remarkable marriages in history.

As Martin Luther instructed the artist to paint his por-
trait "warts and all," so a friend recognizes the blemishes
and accepts them.

Friendship takes time. One feature of romantic love is that
it often takes place in a moment. The scenario goes like
this: "His eyes met hers and they both knew that life

would never again be the same—it was love at first sight." In contrast to this momentary experience, friendship is a slowly ripening fruit—a gradually developing process.

I once met an elderly minister. After some negotiations with him about a real estate matter, I returned home and in my best P.R. style wrote to him saying how much I appreciated his friendship. In his reply he noted my comment, adding significantly, "I certainly hope our relationship will grow into friendship." He was reminding me that friendship takes time.

Romantic love is limited to two people, while friendship encompasses all. Romantic lovers generally have the attitude, "How can we get away from these people and be by ourselves?" Even when in company, they lose sight of all others. Friendship, on the other hand, can involve any number; in fact, the greater the number, the more satisfactory it is likely to become. Friendship is beneficial to the community. Many of the greatest movements in society have begun with a few like-minded people who gathered themselves into some form of association and committed themselves to a common objective.

Romantic love may spawn jealousy, while we delight in sharing our friends. Jealousy is seen as a minus rather than a plus in relationships. Jealousy may be a symptom of guilt. The guilty person may seek justification for inappropriate behavior by seeing his spouse as carrying on in similar activities.

Margaret Mead has noted that women have been called the jealous sex, but it might be more accurate to call them the "insecure sex." Many a woman's economic well-being is dependent upon her husband and so she is relatively easily threatened by a rival who might snatch away not only her husband but also her security.

The jealous person often states the case, "I love you so much I cannot bear to see you with someone else." The philosopher La Rochefoucauld said, "There is more self-love than love in jealousy." The psychoanalyst Fenichel added, "The most jealous persons are those who are not able to love but who need the feeling of being loved."

All of this is in vivid contrast to friendship. We are happy to share our friends with others and delighted when a friend is appreciated by others. Moreover, we are happy to share a friend and to enlarge the friendship circle.

One of the most beautiful pieces of literature in the Bible is the Song of the Bow (1 Sam. 1:17-27) in which a man mourns the passing of his friend. Friendship has also been the key to some of history's classic husband-wife relationships.

Now might be the time for friendship to flower again with the realization that a really good marriage partner is much more than a lover. The woman of earlier times might have been looking for a good provider and a dominant leader. The man might have sought out a good housekeeper or a fertile childbearer. But the hurly-burly of modern-day life demands a marriage which at its best is a union of two friends. The friendship principle might produce the kind of relationship that will make the difference between success and failure in a marriage and provide one of the most significant alternatives to divorce.

The Decisive Motivational Action

1. *Take an inventory of the interests of your spouse and yourself. Notice the way that Mary Anne Disraeli, mentioned in the chapter, listed these traits. See if you can do the same thing.*

MY TRAITS	MY SPOUSE'S TRAITS

2. *List the activities you enjoy by yourself; your spouse enjoys; both of you enjoy together.*

ACTIVITIES I LIKE	ACTIVITIES HE (SHE) LIKES	ACTIVITIES WE LIKE

Do a bit of negotiating. Is there something he does that you could possibly develop an interest in, or vice versa? Try to lengthen the third column.

3. How about friends? Try listing the people you each like, then those you both like.

MY FRIENDS	HIS (HER) FRIENDS	OUR FRIENDS

Consider this listing carefully. How can you lengthen column three? Why not plan to have some of these people in your home? The very activities might have some benefit for your marriage.

Action Strategy #10

TRY RUNNING AROUND

"You don't stop exercising because you are getting old—you get old because you stop exercising."

One of the signs of deteriorating marriage is when one of the partners begins to "run around" on the other. However, there is one type of "stepping out" or "running around" that may benefit a marriage as is seen in the case of Millie Cooper.

Run for Your Life

One night while Millie was watching television with her husband, he asked her to take his resting heartbeat. She checked it at fifty beats a minute. When he tested hers, it was eighty beats a minute. He pointed out that while they slept that night, their two hearts would pump the same amount of blood, but her heart would beat about 10,000 times more frequently than his. With irritating masculine logic, he said, "You're just going to wear out faster than I will."

Millie sat and pondered the situation. Visions of her handsome, trim doctor husband as a widower flitted through her head. She determined to do something about the situation and embarked on an exercise program. Millie Cooper's discovery that exercise and physical fitness were vital to her marriage leads us into a bypath seldom examined when considering the factors that destroy a marriage.

Millie Cooper decided on another plan of action. Although she disliked exercise, she decided the situation called for self-discipline. Mustering all her will power, she started on a regimen of jogging. Millie soon realized it was to become a new way of life, since physical fitness is a continual process.

But it paid off! Describing the benefits derived from her aerobics program, Millie Cooper reported: Her dress size decreased from 12 to 8; she lost ten pounds; her eating habits improved; she enjoyed less tension, better sleeping, an enhanced self-image, and an awareness of her husband's pride in her. All this and longer life, too!

Calories Count

Marian Clark suddenly realized to her dismay that lack of exercise had led her down a dead-end street. Nature had given Marian an exquisitely beautiful face and, as a girl, she was pleasingly plump. When Bill saw her for the first time he was smitten. As he confided to his friend, "She has such a beautiful face, and I like a girl who is a good armful." But following their marriage Marian gradually became several arms' full. As she put on weight, Marian slowed down and spent most of her time sitting. She gained her major satisfactions from eating, thus aggravating the problem.

At work Bill was thrown into the company of several attractive women. Marjorie was trim, well dressed, and vivacious and paid him particular attention. He described his reaction: "I guess I always saw Marian at her worst and Marjorie at her best. The contrast was vivid. I never felt like introducing my wife to my working friends. When she brought the children to work, I left her sitting in my office while I showed the children off to my colleagues. I finally told Marian that if she didn't lose weight, we were headed for divorce."

Of course, if Marian decides to do something about her size, she will have to realize that exercise alone will not solve her weight problem. She must also limit her calorie intake.

Marian is one of a great multitude of people who are on the horns of a dilemma. Obesity may easily be the single most difficult personality problem of our day. Being overweight is a far greater problem than alcoholism or drug addiction. The answer to the problem of alcohol and drugs is simple: Quit. Just give it up altogether. There are many experienced people in the field who feel that this is the only solution. Once an alcoholic or an addict, you cannot suddenly become a moderate user. The situation calls for one supreme act of renunciation.

As unlikely as it seems, obesity is a far more complex problem. No one can completely disavow food. He must eat if he is to survive. His problem is to eat selectively and cautiously. For this, he needs far more will power than the addict or the alcoholic. He is constantly faced with temptation. At least three times a day he must make decisions.

As a housewife, Marian is doubly bedeviled. She must

prepare appetizing food for her family; yet resist the temptation to eat much of it. She is like an alcoholic in a distillery or a drug addict in a dispensary.

Moreover, she will have to be willing to forego one of the great American pastimes—recreational eating. Every social event worthy of note is accompanied by eating. Business is discussed over luncheon. If friends come over for coffee, one feels obligated to offer coffeecake. Special guests are entertained at dinner parties. Even churches have their covered-dish suppers!

Just look around as you enter any good-sized American town and you will see the temples of the new deities—the fast-food industry. No longer are we a people who eat to live, but a people who live to eat—or in the words of the New Testament we have become people "whose God is their belly."

And what does this have to do with the state of marriage? Plenty! A reduced intake of calories and a regular exercise program will make Marian a new woman and offer a live option to divorce. It is often said Americans are digging their graves with their knives and forks. In a case like Marian's, it is not their lives they are burying, but their marriages.

System of Aerobics

Millie Cooper, who managed to get her problem under control and emerged from her program of exercise with a trim figure, a loss of excess weight, a calmer spirit, restful nights, an enhanced self-image and a proud husband, had a good start. Her husband, Kenneth Cooper, is the founder of the Aerobics system—probably the most successful, scientifically based exercise program in existence today.

In one way, Cooper is answering Ponce de Leon. In the year 1513, de Leon landed on Florida's shore in search of the mythical "fountain of youth." The trouble was that he was looking for the wrong substance. He didn't need a liquid but a gas—oxygen. Our need for oxygen is far more important than our need for food. We can survive without food for up to 180 days. We can go without water as long as five to seven days. But without oxygen, our sensitive brain cells die after only six to eight minutes.

About the circulatory system, Dr. Cooper concludes, "Increase its workload, and it increases its efficiency. Sit around and do nothing, and it deteriorates. It's as simple as that." Every movable part of the body needs action. This action should lead to the "training effect" which comes from exercise which produces more blood, more red blood cells, more hemoglobin, more blood plasma, a greater delivery of oxygen, and a much more rapid return and expulsion of wastes.

Traditionally, the heart has been used as a symbol for love. For a long, happily married life the heart is, so to speak, "at the heart of it all."

The heart is not nearly as important in representing a group of emotions as it is at the very physical core of life itself. The center of the intricate circulatory system, this magnificient 10 1/2 ounce pump that we call the heart sends the oxygen-filled blood from the lungs and forces it through the body. Its condition is all-important. Dr. Cooper points out one of the strange anomalies: "Ironically, the heart works faster and less efficiently when you give it little to do than it does when you make more demands upon it. It is a remarkable engine." The big problem we face in our sedentary society is that we make few demands on our heart and, consequently, it becomes flabby. The simplest answer is exercise, planned and vigorously carried out.

Fit To Be Tied?

James Johnson shows another way the fitness issue can affect marriage. James has had a struggle with depression for many years. His wife, Valerie, discovered there is only one thing worse than being depressed and that is living with a depressive. She dreads to see him come home from work, knowing his mood. "He just sits. He doesn't want to talk; doesn't want to go out; doesn't want to do anything. I don't know how I can stand it much longer."

Driven to desperation, Valerie makes an appointment for James to see a psychologist. In the initial interview James is apprehensive. "I guess you'll have me lying on the couch next."

To his surprise Dr. Nelson replies, "Quite the contrary, Mr. Johnson, anything but the couch! We even have some running therapists these days who go jogging with their clients. Jogging is a vital part of their therapy program."

James has been introduced to the important role of exercise in helping people with emotional problems. Joggers speak of the aerobic glow which comes through exercise and helps to give them a new outlook on life.

Dr. Cooper warns that all exercises are not of equal value. To be effective, an exercise must develop the exerciser's aerobic capacity—that is, increase the maximum amount of oxygen his body can process in a given time. Cooper is not impressed with what he calls "passive fitness," which comes from such exercises as body-building techniques. He acknowledges that he does calisthenics himself but admits that these should be considered the bricks on the top rather than the foundation of an exercise program. From his wide experience, Cooper has developed a very simple hierarchy of desirable exercises—running and jogging, swimming, cycling, stationary running, walking.

Probably his greatest contribution to the world of physical exercise is Cooper's technique for quantifying the amount of exercise an individual needs. He has done this with a points system. The desirable state of the "conditioned" person is to do exercises that earn thirty points a week. To accomplish this, an individual may walk three miles in no more than forty-one minutes, five times a week; swim 700 yards in fifteen minutes, five times a week; run a mile in eight minutes, twice a week.[1]

Some people with a rather fatalistic view of life claim every individual has a certain number of allotted heartbeats during his lifetime. When he has used up this number, it is the end of the road. Even if we accept this premise, the best way to stave off the last "lub dub" is not by resting but by exercising. As one exercise enthusiast put it, "You don't stop exercising because you are getting old, you are getting old because you stop exercising."

Play Together and Stay Together

Exercise may be the secret of a long life, but will it be worth living? To add quality to the quantity of life, husbands and wives might learn to exercise together.

Such activities as swimming and tennis come to mind. My wife and I enjoy bicycling. We both own individual bikes but decided to buy a tandem for our exercise program. We soon discovered that riding tandem was quite different from riding individual bikes.

Even mounting the bike is done with a different technique. Robina in the back (in cycling jargon, the "stoker" as opposed to the "captain" who steers the front) soon found that if she mounted first, there was always a good chance I would give her a kick in the solar plexus as I swung my leg over the bike frame. Similarly, in dismounting, Robina had to be off first while I steadied the bike. Once underway, I had a clear view of the pathway ahead and so became the lookout.

In short order we developed a new language to use in communicating with each other. Such words included *bump* when a ridge appeared in the road; *lift* when one of those bone-shattering chuckholes loomed ahead; *downing* when necessary to reduce speed; *ease up* when one partner was pushing too hard. Negotiating a corner called for special teamwork. Although I controlled the front wheel, bikes are turned by leaning to the right or left. If Robina decided to turn one way and I the other, it could be disastrous. Similarly, Robina gave all the hand signals while I concentrated on keeping us on course. When we really learned to work together and keep the channels of communication open, we went spinning along.

But our conversation isn't limited to the mechanics of navigation and cycling. We discuss houses, lawns, trees, dogs friendly or hostile, things having to do with our family. We have met other cyclists and various other hardy souls who brave the 6:00 A.M. darkness to get some exercise. The supreme bonus is the feeling of well-being when, after an hour of cycling, we shower, sit down to breakfast, and open our Bibles and hearts to talk with Almighty God.

A good exercise program will benefit your marriage in a number of different ways. It will give you more years of married life together. It will improve your mental and emotional outlook. One medical doctor claims, "There is a mood elevation which lasts for six to eighteen hours after exercise." The third benefit comes from an improved love life. One researcher claims that people who are physically fit spend longer periods making love, as much as an hour compared with the average of about seventeen minutes. The frequency of lovemaking also increases. Those who are physically fit are "seven-day-a-week people."

The Decisive Motivational Action

EXERCISE

1. *Don't overlook the possibilities in ordinary activities of life. One expert has suggested the shopping expedition can be an exercise experience—reaching down to lower shelves, twisting around for an item, carrying out the sacks of groceries.*

2. *Three good principles for incorporating activity into life:*
   - *Don't lie when you can sit.*
   - *Don't sit when you can stand.*
   - *Don't stand when you can move.*

3. *A good program of exercise requires a decisive motivational effort of at least twenty minutes a day. Exercise for four or five minutes a day will not accomplish very much.*

4. *Develop your exercise program gradually. The Greeks had a myth about a man who picked up a calf and carried it. He continued lifting the calf daily and as the calf grew, so did his strength. Get the message? Do it gradually.*

5. *Exercise regularly. Some studies show that unexercised muscles deteriorate at a rapid rate. After three days of immobility, an individual loses as much as 1/5 of his maximum muscle strength. One study by NASA scientists shows daily exercise is preferable, but if this is not possible, exercise on three non-consecutive days each week will maintain an adequate level of fitness.*

6. *Exercise sensibly. If your breathing has not returned to normal within five to ten minutes after exercising, there is a good chance you may be overdoing it.*

7. However, exercise need not dominate your life. Rationalize it into your lifestyle. I ride a stationary bike each morning and put in the thirty minutes watching two courses on Sunrise Semester. I accumulate my "points" and have learned a lot at the same time.

8. Read the book **Aerobics** by Kenneth Cooper.

Action Strategy #11

LEARN TO LISTEN

"Communication is a chain of events."

Isn't it ridiculous the way husbands and wives experience difficulties relating to each other? It certainly shows that the institution of marriage is not what it's cracked up to be. It might well be that we'll have to rethink the whole thing.

Well, yes and no.

I once took an organized overseas tour which provided, not only a contact with other cultures, but also a fascinating study of the effects of close living on interpersonal relationships.

Two middle-aged sisters, reared in a fine family, had been very close to each other through the years. In many ways the tour was, for them, a return to the days of their girlhood. But after three weeks of traveling on a bus and sharing a room, they had a difference of opinion which left their relationship in a state of disrepair for the remainder of the trip.

Two men, a bachelor and a widower, business associates for a long period, had eagerly anticipated their experiences as roommates on the tour. Two weeks out, after one hectic and tiring day, they went to their motel room to become embroiled in a violent disagreement over who was going to sleep in the bed with the reading lamp. Following this altercation, they maintained a resolute posture of silence toward each other and caused the whole tour group to align themselves as either the "Harry" or "Ken" backers.

As a psychologist I speculated about the immaturity of these adults and what I could do to bring some rationality into the situation. Then one day we were eating in a crowded Dutch hotel. Baldheaded Mr. Harrison had managed to gain possession of the solitary saltshaker. Instead of handing it over in response to my plea, he passed it to his own little clique. As I sat there eating my insipid food, I darkly conjured a "pretend" plot to organize a block of fellow tourists against him.

If a group of well-educated people, living in close quarters for a month, found it difficult to adjust, it is something of a feat that some couples live together day in and day out for many years with few serious differences.

Just One Thing After Another

Communication itself is a chain of events—a step-by-step process. Understanding the steps gives us some clues as to where husband-and-wife communication goes astray.

The case of Helen White provides a starting point. Helen tells her husband, Bruce, that she feels the housekeeping budget should be increased. She reinforces her case with an *information source*—the reports of friends' housekeeping budgets and the amount of money Bruce saves for his biannual hunting trips. Helen proceeds to *encode* her message—she takes great care in choosing the words she uses to discuss this touchy subject. Bruce frequently complains that Helen speaks too softly, so she *transmits* her message by raising the volume of her voice. The message moves along the *channel*, traveling from Helen's mouth to Bruce's ears.

As the *receiver*, Bruce looks straight at Helen so he can both see and hear her in order to understand the message. Bruce is busily engaged in *decoding*—trying to make sure he understands what Helen means as she sprinkles her statements with such expressions as "sky-high prices," "staples," and "mad money." The message arrives at its *destination*—Bruce's brain. He evaluates Helen's proposition and weighs the pros and cons of increasing the housekeeping allowance.

Though this may sound fairly simple, it is actually an oversimplification of an infinitely complex operation which, like all complicated procedures, can easily get out of gear. The main problem comes from the nature of the communication experience. Because it is a chain of events, it is possible for communication to break down at any one or more of the links. Beginning in a husband or wife's brain and following in sequence until the destination of the spouse's brain is reached, the process can easily be disrupted at a number of sensitive spots which we will call *distortion points*. Because a chain is only as strong as its weakest link, each of these points is of the greatest significance.

Seven possible distortion points can be seen in this incident:

- As Helen thinks about her situation, she may have some wrong ideas—Type A Distortion.

- When she puts her thoughts into words, she may make the wrong choice—Type B Distortion.

- As she speaks, she could make an emphasis that would change the meaning—Type C Distortion.

- The children may be making a noise that will interfere with the message as it passes from Helen's lips to Bruce's ears—Type D Distortion.

- Bruce's hearing may not be the best and may give rise to a Type E Distortion.

- Puzzling over some of his wife's expressions like "mad money" Bruce may experience Type F Distortion.

- As Bruce considers the proposition, a Type G Distortion may complicate the message.

This brief description illustrates the complexity of husband-wife communication. To say merely that a husband and wife have a communication problem, is a gross oversimplification.

We will need to consider the seven distortion points which may aggravate a husband-wife relationship and ultimately lead them into the divorce court.

What Did You Expect?

We have already noted in Chapter 3 that many people have confused ideas and expectations as they enter into marriage. These confused expectations easily lead to foul-ups in communication.

Wanda Harrison is dabbing her face in an effort to save something of the make-up she had applied earlier in the day. Her husband is gently holding her in his arms to comfort her. This was their first big fuss in twelve months of marriage. Now they are in the process of making-up, and both feel a little foolish about the experience, inwardly resolving it will never happen again.

Between sniffles and dabs, Wanda speaks, "It was my fault. I always thought husbands *liked* to bring their wives coffee in bed."

"I always thought."

Probably no experience in life is entered upon with such high expectations as is marriage, and husband and wife generally believe remarkable things are going to happen to them in this relationship. Their ideas have come from a number of sources—friends, parents, relatives, TV, novels—and many of these are bound to be false.

- "*I always thought* wives got up early to prepare breakfast for their husbands."
- "*I always thought* my husband would never look at another woman."
- "*I always thought* our marriage would be like a perpetual honeymoon."

In these expressions we confront an axiom of communication: *There is a difference between fact and opinion.* The "I always thought" comes from the conviction of some people that they know all there is to be known about a subject.

How will we handle communication problems coming from confused thinking?

1. *Develop humility.* When a professor of mathematics from the City University of New York went to visit the great scientist, Einstein, he approached him apprehensively. After explaining that he had some ideas he would like to discuss, Einstein responded by inviting him to put the equations on a chalkboard, adding, "Please go slowly—I don't understand things quickly."

A little ditty puts it like this, "All things I thought I knew but now confess—the more I know I know, I know I know the less." We must always remain open to the possibility of new information on the subject.

2. *Because it is clear to you, it doesn't follow that your spouse will automatically understand.* You may feel you know what your spouse "should" know, but there is a good chance you don't.

3. *Try a "which" pinpoint.*
"Wives always get up early to fix breakfast for their husbands."
Which wives?
Which husbands?
"A husband would never even glance at another woman."
Which husband?
Which woman?

The computer people have given us the word *Gigo*—"Garbage in, garbage out." This applies not only to computers but to marriages. When a married couple begin talking to each other, they must have adequate information or the communication will be stillborn—die in its birth.

The Words We Use

As the Pioneer 10 spacecraft soared aloft from Cape Kennedy on its journey to the space beyond the solar system, it carried a six-by-nine plaque. Engraved on the plaque was what has now come to be known as a "message from earth." According to the NASA release this plaque was "designed to show scientifically educated inhabitants of some other star system who might intercept it millions of years from now—when Pioneer 10 was launched, from where, and by what kind of beings."

In a test, a copy of this plaque was shown to over one hundred people, all college graduates, some with doctor's degrees. *Not one* of them was able to decipher the message. If these erudite scientists had so little success in devising a way of communicating their ideas to the residents of outer space, it is small wonder that husbands and wives have problems in passing on their ideas to each other.

This type of distortion is also found in the *ambivalent*

messages husbands and wives give each other. The problem comes when a spouse wants to get a message across to a mate. Not wishing to come straight out and say it, he sends two messages—what he feels will be acceptable to his spouse and what he really thinks.

Mrs. Marsh has news for her husband. "Mother would like us to spend our vacation with them this year. Don't you think that would be a good idea?"

Bob Marsh replies, "That's fine. Kind of her to invite us. My problem is that the boss says I may have to delay my vacation this year. It's not at all certain, but there's just enough doubt to make it impossible for me to make specific plans. Of course, if you'd like to go on your own. . ."

Bob is telling his wife that he doesn't want to upset her, but he's not going to visit his in-laws for the vacation. This type of communication is sometimes referred to as a "double message" and wreaks havoc with interpersonal communication.

Then there is the communication distortion known as *nagging*. Nagging fails as a communication technique because of the familiarity of the material.

The word *nag* has been defined as "To torment by persistent fault-finding, complaints, or importunities." The Oxford Dictionary adds some interesting overtones to the definition, stating that to nag means "to gnaw, bite, nibble." Most husbands and wives become defensive or completely ignore the nagger.

If you are tempted to nag, here are some hints for avoiding the temptation:

1. Don't make a predictable response.

2. Remember, no matter what satisfaction it gives you, nagging has a negative influence, so you've accomplished nothing.

3. Be subtle. Get your idea across in as many different ways as you can.

4. Acknowledge that you don't know everything and that you could just be wrong.

5. Build the logic of your ideas so the family will be able to reach some conclusions of their own.

6. Don't gloat when logic proves you to be correct.

The Way You Say It Makes The Difference

Linda Simpson is pouring out a tearful story to her mother. Mrs. Stacey has never suspected there might be difficulties in her daughter's marriage. Though anxious to be loyal to her own flesh and blood, she wonders if her daughter may not be exaggerating.

Mrs. Stacey is particularly bothered by the vague complaint, "I never thought he would talk to me like that," and asks gently, "Tell me exactly what Tom said."

Linda dabs her tears and responds, "It wasn't so much what he said as the hateful *way he said it*."

Linda has run upon the technique whereby the meaning of a statement can be changed by the manner in which it is spoken.

The method of speaking can also be used to make a critical message more palatable. This technique was used by a gifted psychotherapist working in therapy groups using confrontational methods. He masked his incisive mind behind an engaging smile. As the session progressed, the time came for him to do some confronting. He launched into the process of facing a group member with some negative aspects of his adjustment to life.

The therapist turned his beaming countenance upon the subject and, in a voice sounding for all the world like a fond parent expressing loving disappointment, made the frankest statements: "That certainly was a childish action to take." "You have obviously been very irresponsible." "You didn't show up too well there." His face continued to be wreathed in a winning smile. Very seldom did anybody take umbrage at the statements that would have normally made them hopping mad. The expression on his face and the note of concern in his voice made all the difference in passing on the message.

Joseph Conrad, skillful craftsman of literature and word wizard, is credited with saying, "Give me the right word and the right accent, and I will move the world." Communication does not exist in words alone. The manner in which the message is transmitted can make all the difference.

Blocking the Flow Between Husband and Wife

Far too many husbands and wives fail to build and maintain a communication base. Conversation is a lost art.

If you want to see how badly the conversational art has deteriorated, just peek in on a husband and wife having dinner out in the restaurant. Observe the couples who are looking into each other's eyes and carrying on a spirited conversation—they're not married.

On the other hand, if they give the appearance of being a couple of strangers that the maitre d' has fitted in at the same table and if they are silently working their way through the meal, there's a good chance they're husband

and wife. Bound by a solemn marriage vow, they are conversationally separated from each other by a great chasm.

The art of conversation requires both thought and effort on the part of the participants, but it's an art that once mastered will enrich a husband-wife relationship.

One conversation stopper is the put-down response. Some of these are just space-fillers, but others give the speaker the satisfaction of having made a clever response. Put-downs include:

- *"I know I'm wasting my breath, but . . ."*
- *"No one in his right mind could believe that . . ."*
- *"Everybody knows that . . ."*
- *"Where did you get that dumb idea?"*
- *"It really isn't any of my business, but . . ."*
- *"Why do you always think you know more than anybody else?"*
- *"If you're not interested in hearing the facts . . ."*
- *"Are you trying to be funny?"*
- *"I don't want to hurt your feelings, but . . ."*
- *"If I tell you something, will you promise not to get mad?"*

You can take one of two attitudes toward put-downs. You can cherish the moment of ego inflation in having been clever. Or you can take a long look and ask yourself if this will really strengthen your relationship. By forgoing your ego trip, you will be moving toward better interaction rather than derailing your conversational partner.

If you feel the interaction between you and your spouse is slowing down, why not try some conversational stimulators?

- *Help your spouse to save face. People often make foolish statements which are obviously incorrect; you don't have to correct your partner—keep listening.*

- *Be as pleasant and friendly with your husband or wife as you would with a stranger, and don't forget to listen.*
- *People are always more interested in themselves than they are in you—so listen.*
- *As your spouse talks, formulate a question that will encourage him or her and then listen for the answer.*
- *Play conversational tennis, seeing how adept you can become in hitting the conversational ball back to your mate and wait for a return by listening.*
- *Watch for warning signals; be sensitive to your partner's reactions. If you are not doing so well, try listening for awhile.*

Franklin D. Roosevelt led his country through World War II with a unique communication style. A conversationalist of the highest order, he used conversational power to rally the nation.

This style contrasted vividly with that of Winston Churchill, the other famous World War II leader. Both of them used the radio, but while Churchill delivered his grandiloquent orations, Roosevelt chose an intimate method in the messages referred to as "Fireside Chats."

In these conversations Roosevelt put himself into the role of a father talking to his children. The nation was one large family and daddy sat by the fire, opened his heart to his people and shared the national problems with them. He consciously tried to visualize that family. One who observed him in action noted, "His head would nod and his hands move in simple, natural gestures. His face would light up as though he were actually sitting on the front porch or in the parlor with them."

In his face-to-face meetings with people, President Roosevelt was equally charming. He had the capacity to make people feel important by the way he listened and responded to what they said.

Frank Capra, the celebrated movie producer, spent some time with the president and describes the way in which he entered into a conversation. "With a big friendly smile and the glint of intense interest in his sparkling eyes, he would encourage you to talk about yourself, your family, your work, anything. 'Well, I declare!' he'd exclaim after you'd made some inane statement. By little laughs and goads and urgings such as 'Really? Tell me more!' . . . 'Well, what do you know!' . . . 'Same thing's happened to me dozens of times!' . . . 'Oh, that's fascinating' . . . his warmth would change you from a stuttering milquetoast to an articulate raconteur."

Small wonder that President Roosevelt, the man of the people, was able to marshall the forces of democracy against the tyranny of the Axis powers.

The Roosevelt method will work for you. Listen for interesting responses. Make a list and memorize them; then when the moment comes, try them out. Notice the way in which they stimulate and enrich communication.

Will You Hear What Is Said?

A man who serves in the U.S. Army lays his life on the line in wartime. Despite excellent medical services he may suffer injuries that will incapacitate him for the rest of his days. Yet, the gravest danger he faces is not mutilation or death—but *loss of hearing!*

That's right. Your ears are not deceiving you. U.S. Army authorities report that noise-induced hearing loss may be the single greatest occupational hazard for all combat troops. It has been conservatively estimated that from 30 to 50 percent of all active duty army personnel suffer some noise-induced hearing loss during their military careers. The wife of an artillery man, a tanker, or infantry man may discover her husband often fails to hear what she says.

The experience isn't peculiar to the military. The barriers to people "hearing" each other are not always physical. Sometimes there is a negative *anticipatory set* when husbands and wives communicate.

One television show has popularized a game in which husbands and wives are separated from each other. In turn, both the husband and wife are asked to say what they believe their mates' ideas are on a given subject or how they they will respond to a certain situation. In an unusual number of cases, the answer is wrong.

These experiences are an example of the basic false assumption of marriage: Most husbands and wives believe they have a clear insight into their spouse's mental processes and reactions. This just *isn't* true.

Whenever I hear a woman say, "My husband believes . . . ." my instant reaction is, "I wonder what he would think if he could hear this statement."

Steve Casey, talking with his wife, braces himself and says, "Okay. Go ahead. Get it off your chest. But I already know what you're going to say."

He puts on the appearance of a householder battening down for a hurricane and waits defiantly for her argument. The "anticipatory set" means many a message from a spouse is cut off at the receiver level.

Emotional factors like *guilt* may cause a communication breakdown as is seen in the biblical incident of Amnon and Tamar. Amnon, attracted to his beautiful half-sister, finally trapped her in his house and raped her. Following the episode he cast her out of the house. The Bible tells us that before the event Amnon "loved her"; following the sexual episode, "Amnon hated her exceedingly; so that the hatred wherewith he hated her was greater than the love wherewith he had loved her" (2 Sam. 13:15, KJV). The guilt of his act caused a complete change in Amnon's perception of Tamar.

Handling guilt may help clarify communication. A good series of steps is:

1. Be willing to sit down and ruthlessly examine the situation.

2. Accept responsibility. Put aside your ego defenses and accept whatever blame belongs to you.

3. Become open—acknowledge failure—to yourself, another person, significant others.

4. Undertake some act of restitution. Put things right if you have hurt someone.

You Heard But Did You Listen?

Mr. Henry is in a towering rage. Before he departed on his most recent business trip, he'd given his son, Ted, a long lecture on the importance of watering his prize orchids. As he was given the instructions, Mr. Henry was vaguely aware of Ted's casual attitude which said in effect, "Sure, Pop, just leave it to me."

On his return, Mr. Henry had hurried out to the greenhouse to find his precious plants wilted, positive evidence of Ted's neglect. As the elder Henry proceeded to pour out his wrath, his son sat looking rather like some martyr being persecuted for his faith.

As Mr. Henry noticed his son's somewhat benign countenance, something snapped. At this moment, vividly aware of all his offspring's irresponsibilities and failures, he yelled, "Do you hear me?"

Of course, the boy heard him. The whole household heard him. Even the neighbors across the street heard him. The problem was that Ted didn't *listen* to his father. If communication is to take place, there must be a listener.

We have followed the journey of a message across six distortion points from the brain of one individual to the brain of another person. This process is complex and involved. We might now imagine that the message reaching the brain would bring forth the intended purpose of the speaker. Unfortunately, the greatest hurdle is that the receiver may not be listening. If you are to get the message, you cannot listen with your ears alone but also read visually by concentrating on the speaker.

If you are going to be an effective listener, you must give the speaker your undivided attention. It is his moment, and every aspect of your demeanor must say, "Come on. Let's have it. You're in the center of the stage in my thinking."

The counselor who must be a good listener doesn't do a lot of things. He does not lean back in his chair with eyes half closed and none of those furtive looks as if mentally cataloging the books on his shelves. He doesn't steal glances at his watch with the inference, "Time is up; you've been here long enough." He doesn't idly doodle on a pad.

The good listener is relaxed. The telephone is cared for; his secretary warned against interruptions. He leans slightly toward the speaker, his eyes focused on him, not in a staring match, but in a coaxing, interested manner. Every aspect of the listening one says, "Tell me more."

Husband and wives who hope to improve communication better learn how to listen. Take a cue from the marriage counselor. The "tell me more" attitude may spark new understanding and open up a whole new dimension in marriage relations.

The Decisive Motivational Action

In Chapter 4 we discussed contracts. The following is a communication contract. It might be a good idea to recall the principles laid down in Chapter 6 as ground rules for a good communication experience.

1. No attempts to go back over past history.
2. No "zaps."
3. No blaming.
4. No threats or ultimatums.

COMMUNICATION CONTRACT

We the undersigned, being parties to this agreement, each hereby agree:

I AGREE communication is the basic of a good marriage relationship, and I will embark on a course of action to build up our interpersonal communications.

I AGREE that I will listen to your remarks and comments without interrupting you. When it is my turn to talk, I expect the same courtesy.

I AGREE that I will first look for things to criticize about myself before I criticize you. Before I complain to you, I will name some fault of mine that, if corrected, would make me a better marriage partner.

I AGREE that sex is a significant level of communication and that I have a sexual obligation in our marriage. Our sexual relations will never be used as a means of reward or punishment.

I AGREE that direct communication is desirable, and I will try not to use ambivalent language or talk through the children, but specifically say what I mean.

I AGREE that communication proceeds best on a verbal level, and I will not try to send messages by banging doors or other nonverbal means.

I AGREE not to use silence as a means of punishing or defying you but as a means of encouraging you to express yourself.

I AGREE not to expect miracles in the improvement of our marriage. There is a great deal you need to know about me and I about you before we can consider ourselves truly married. But I will make every effort toward mutual knowledge and understanding.

I AGREE on the assumption that example is the most persuasive form of argument known to man, that I will deligently seek to improve myself and my communication skills so I can grow into a continually better model of a marriage mate.

Husband_____

Date_____   Wife_____

Action Strategy #12

GET HELP

"Listen to my counsel—oh don't refuse it—and be wise."
SOLOMON (Prov. 8:33, TLB)

"Our parents didn't go running off to a counselor every time they had a little disagreement," John Harrison retorted when his wife suggested that they should discuss their marital difficulties with a professional counselor.

To those like John who imagine marriage counseling is a new-fangled idea, it will probably come as something of a surprise to discover that counseling was an established practice as far back as 1000 years before Christ. The counselors were known as wise men and they sat at the gates of the city where troubled people came by to air their problems.

The wise men listened to the problem and then quoted a proverb that was applicable to the individual situation. Many of these proverbs have been preserved and tell us about the types of problems faced by the people of those ancient times.

1 "A virtuous woman is a crown to her husband: but she that maketh ashamed is as rottenness in his bones" (Prov. 12:4, KJV).

2 "It is better to live in the corner of an attic than with a crabby woman in a lovely home" (Prov. 21:9, TLB).

"A rebellious son is a calamity to his father, and a nagging wife annoys like constant dripping" (Prov. 19:13, TLB).

"A rebellious son is a grief to his father and a bitter blow to his mother" (Prov. 17:25, TLB).

3 "The fool who provokes his family to anger and resentment will finally have nothing worthwhile left. He shall be the servant of a wiser man" (Prov. 11:29, TLB).

From these proverbs we learn that people have always had personal problems, they talked about their problems with wise men and many of their problems concerned marriage relationships.

The Distress Signals of Marriage

No marriage is perfect. It is the union of two imperfect people. Therefore, it follows that there will be rough spots along the way. For many people marriage requires just a little flexibility and willingness to adjust. Professional help is not necessary. However, for other marriages there comes a time when husband and wife realize the situation is beyond their control.

How do we know when we need professional help? The following ten distress signals may give us some clues:

1. Frequent arguments that never seem to solve problems.

2. A feeling of disappointment because there seems to be a disparity in what you expect from your marriage and what you are getting.

3. A feeling that your spouse is making greater demands on you than you can or want to respond to.

4. A lack of enjoyment and pleasure in your spouse's company—even to the point that you dislike him or her.

5. Avoiding being alone with your spouse by constantly visiting friends or going places by yourself.

6. A feeling of loneliness, isolation, or depression that drives you to frequently discuss your marriage problems with others.

7. Overuse of sleeping pills, tranquilizers, or other drugs.

8. Constant fatigue without cause.

9. An inability to obtain sexual fulfillment.

10. Persistent problems with children, such as their constantly getting into serious trouble.

Notice there are ten of these signals. Most marriages will experience problems related to one or more. If you experience several of these signals, it may be an indication that you need to seek outside help with your marriage.

To Whom Do You Go?

Life grows more complex with passing time. In this space age, home and family life is beset with more difficulties. A group of professionals have emerged to help heal the hurts of troubled people, including the more intimate relationships between husband and wife. Professionals qualified as marriage counselors include ministers, psychiatrists, psychologists, social workers, and marriage counselors. They come from a variety of backgrounds and use different techniques. Consequently, if you want to go to a counselor you need to know something about the work he or she can do.

A psychiatrist is a medical doctor who, in addition to his medical training, has completed a psychiatric internship. This training prepares him to deal with major emotional abnormalities. If there are indications that one or both of the spouses are psychotic—out of touch with reality, hallucinating, hearing voices, seeing objects, smelling smells that are not obvious to anybody else, or delusional with utterly false ideas, they will probably need the help of a psychiatrist. However, if the two parties are functioning normally, but having difficulty relating to each other, they probably don't need psychiatric help. Remember, too, a psychiatrist's fees are pretty steep, although some fees are covered by medical insurance.

Social workers with adequate training generally hold a master's degree (M.S.W.) earned after graduating from college with a B.A. degree. The social worker's training can be in several areas. One who has training in marriage counseling will probably be able to help with your marriage difficulties.

A psychologist holds a Ph.D., an Ed.D., or D.Psy. degree. If a psychologist has served in an internship, he is generally referred to as a Clinical Psychologist. In many states psychologists must be certified and licensed. Nevertheless, not all psychologists even though certified, and licensed, have training in marriage counseling.

The title "marriage counselor" is loosely used to describe any of the previously mentioned professionals. But there is now a group of professionals accredited by the American Association for Marriage and Family Therapists.

Modern theological education places a great emphasis on preparing ministers for a counseling ministry. Ministers are frequently excellent counselors because of their interest in people. Many ministers are committed to helping husbands and wives find fulfillment in their marriage relationship. Some ministers belong to professional organizations such as The Association of Pastoral Counselors, or participate in training generally referred to as Clinical Pastoral Education. A minister is an obvious starting point for a troubled couple. If ministers cannot handle a situation they will be able to refer you to someone who can help.

Self-help groups can provide help for many of the problem areas of marriages. The oldest and best known is Alcoholics Anonymous, and it is still probably the most effective help available for alcoholics, their wives and their relatives. The number for Alcoholics Anonymous is generally listed in the telephone directory. Don't overlook Alanon for husbands and wives or Alateen for teenage children.

Self-help groups operate on the principle that "like helps like." Some groups offering their help are: Gamblers

Anonymous, Neurotics Anonymous, and Overweights Anonymous. One particularly helpful group is Integrity Therapy which is called "AA in civilian dress." People training in Integrity Therapy make some special applications to the problems of home and family life.

Our overview hasn't even scratched the surface of the wide variety of services available for helping people with difficulties in their marriage or family life. Consequently, a husband or wife seeking counseling may have some difficulty in deciding just where to go. Use the following criteria to evaluate a counselor:

1. Does this counselor make great claims of success with his counseling? If so, watch out. A really good counselor will acknowledge his failures, but is anxious to be of help.

2. Does this counselor have adequate preparation? Check his credentials, particularly his practical experience. Don't be afraid to ask about his qualifications.

3. Have you talked with someone who has used the practitioner's services? Even though thoroughly trained, he or she may not relate well to some people. If you can get an assessment of the counselor from a counselee's perspective, it will help in making a good choice.

4. Is this person a professing Christian? In such areas as marriage, ethical questions are sure to arise. If the counselor has Christian convictions, you will have a better basis on which to build your interchange.

5. Is this counselor available at a convenient time? Experience in one center has shown that a reluctant husband has a built-in excuse to avoid counseling if it is only available during the day. Some counseling centers offer counseling in the evening hours for the convenience of working people.

6. What are the fees for counseling? Psychiatric consultation will probably be the most expensive. At the other end of the continuum, Alcoholics Anonymous does not charge at all. Any established agency will have a scale of fees based on the client's ability to pay. Most counselors will not turn anybody away because of lack of money.

Group or Individual Counseling?

In some counseling centers you will be given the opportunity for either individual or group counseling. Some people think of counseling as a traumatic experience. Remind yourself that all group counseling is not the same. Talk to someone who has participated in a particular group before making a choice.

After working for many years as a counselor, I am convinced that there are advantages in group counseling.

Group counseling highlights relationships. The whole process of personality development begins with relationships formed with family members. As development takes place, one learns to cope with increasingly greater numbers of people. Most of the troubles encountered in life come from difficulties in relationships. And even in marriage, the problems stem from your relationship to a spouse or other members of the family.

Removing yourself from contact with people results in isolation. If you're going to be helped, it will mean that the process must be reversed. A one-to-one counseling experience certainly provides a starting point for this reversal, but no more than that. The counseling group becomes the means by which the counselee enters into a whole new series of relationships and develops basic relationship skills.

A good counseling group builds trust and confidence. You may not be enthusiastic about the idea of group counseling. You may have the idea that your case is peculiar and can only be dealt with on an individual basis. You may see a group as a challenge to your attitude about people and relationships. This could be an indication of one reason why you may need group counseling.

Some people argue, "I cannot talk in the presence of a group; it would be impossible for me to bare my soul before a number of other people." Yet, one counseling center which had functioned on a one-to-one basis for a long period discovered that people are more open before a group than they are in one-to-one counseling. Many women, particularly, were able to discuss very intimate and personal matters more freely than they ever did in individual counseling.

When you join a group you will probably hear about a covenant of confidentiality. It is an assurance that the group members have no desire to exploit you, only to help. If you formerly looked upon every new acquaintance with a questioning eye, now you may come to have faith in a group of people who are concerned about you and listen intently whenever you speak. Gradually, you will discover that you are building an attitude of trust toward others. This may be exactly what you need if you have been hurt by some of the incidents of home and family life.

Groups frequently build self-esteem. In a good group you will soon discover that you can help someone else. If you have a capable leader, he will utilize you in the group processes in such a way that even though you may not have your own problem completely under control, you will discover that you can help someone else. As you make your first feeble efforts at helping another person, you will probably be aware of new abilities. Your self-esteem will probably grow. Life will begin to look better. In helping someone else, you will help yourself.

Group experiences provide feedback. In the process of presenting your problem to the group, you will encounter a variety of reactions and feedback from the other members. Because of these responses you will be able to see your difficulties from a number of different points of view. This enables you to take a look at them from a new perspective.

I was invited to join a group of educators on a regular weekly panel program. We worked hard preparing what we hoped would be a model for programs to follow. Our work led to preparation of scripts and teaching aids, with long discussions about the most effective ways of getting our ideas across. After many false starts, the program was finally videotaped. Following the taping, the program director took us to a room where the technicians played back our program. As we watched the videotape it became a moment of humiliating truth for me—as with sinking stomach I saw the way I appeared on that wretched video tube. I journeyed home that night with the conviction that I was a complete flop as a television performer and needed to rethink my whole television technique.

The director responsible for the program taught us a valuable lesson without saying a single word. Seeing ourselves as we appeared to other people proved to be a powerful teacher.

Feedback is a major function of group interaction. When

you join a group there is a sense of entering a hall of mirrors and gradually coming to see yourself through a variety of self-images. Some of these images may be disturbing at first. One basic principle has emerged from many behavioral studies: The more knowledge of results we receive about our performance, the greater is our learning. One of the greatest benefits of being in a group may be the feedback experiences it provides.

Group counseling provides experiences of interaction. As you enter the group you will discover that the leader works at bringing all the members into contact with each other. If isolation is the biggest problem you face, a group will stimulate you to reach out to others.

How Does It Look From The Inside?

The foregoing represents the conclusion of a psychologist observing what happens in group counseling. But how does it look from the perspective of someone who is a member of a group?

Fortunately for us, a psychiatrist specializing in group psychotherapy has written an authoritative work on the subject. In a survey to discover just how people perceived their group experience, they were given sixty statements about group therapy reactions. They were asked to select the ones that most nearly reflected their experiences. The ten items considered the most significant were:

1. Discovering and accepting previously unknown or unacceptable parts of myself.

2. Being able to say what was bothering me instead of holding it in.

3. Other members honestly telling me what they think of me.

✓4. Learning how to express my feelings.

5. The group's teaching me about the type of impression I make on others.

✓6. Expressing negative and/or positive feelings toward another member.

✓7. Learning that I must take ultimate responsibility for the way I live my life no matter how much guidance and support I get from others.

8. Learning how I come across to others.

9. Seeing that others could reveal embarrassing things and take other risks helped me to do the same.

10. Feeling more trustful of groups and of other people.

This unsolicited testimonial may help you to understand better how group counseling "comes across" to people who participate in the experience.

In July, 1977 a man walked out of a house in Spain and shielded his eyes against the glare of the unfamiliar sun. His snow-white hair and alabaster skin bore evidence to many years lived in the cellar of his house. Now 77 years old, el Senor Protasio had once been the socialist mayor of the mountain resort town of Cercedilla. When Generalissimo Francisco Franco's Nationalist forces took over the village, Protasio Montalvo first hid in his house and then dug a cellar. He stayed there for 38 years. He whiled away the time by feeding crumbs to the sparrows and teaching tricks to successive generations of dogs. Asked why he had remained so long in his cellar, he replied, "Only now did I think it was safe." So the socialist who professed a philosophy that was to change the world spent half his life, a period in which some of the greatest social upheavals of all time were taking place, cowering in a cellar. Participation in group counseling can be compared to Protasio's seclusion—it involves a certain risk, a willingness to interact with others. We must decide whether we want to be safe, feeding sparrows and training dogs, or to take the risks that are part of life.

The Art of Being Counseled

Counseling is not something that is done *to* a person. At best it provides an experience in which you make decisions about yourself, face the alternatives that are open to you, anticipate what will happen if you follow these alternatives, and then decide on what actions you need to take. You will get out of counseling only what you are willing to put into it.

Make sure you are going to the right place. Several widows and divorcees have come to our counseling center looking for new husbands. They heard the center helped people who were having difficulties. Their difficulties centered around their need for a husband. We had to inform them that they had come to the wrong place. We were not a "lonely hearts club." Make sure that you go to the right place.

Call or make an appointment. Don't be afraid to ask the receptionist about fees, lengths of session, or number of sessions generally needed.

If your husband (or wife) will not go with you, it may still be beneficial to go by yourself. The counselor may be able to help you work out ways to encourage your spouse to participate.

When you sit down to talk with the counselor, remember that the focus of the discussion will be you and your problems. This is not a social visit. It is an effort to help you with your problems. Don't waste your time talking about trivia.

Be prepared to be open about your relationship with your spouse. Openness is: not complaining, not blaming other people for your problems and your difficulty, and not telling the counselor about all your strengths and outstanding characteristics. Don't be afraid to talk about your weaknesses and failures.

Don't spend your time talking about other people's failures. Focus on your own.

Trust your counselor. He is there to help you.

Don't get upset because a session might not come up to your expectations. Things may not always go the way you want them. Remember, it took a long time for your difficulties to build up and it's going to take time for you to work through them.

There is one concluding precaution. In much the same way as someone who reads a medical book wonders if he is suffering from a number of illnesses, it is possible to become too introspective about a marriage relationship. You may have such high expectations about the experiences marriage should be providing, that you feel you must see a marriage counselor. But in trying to state your problem, all you can say is, "Our marriage is not as good as it could be." No marriage is. The good counselor will be able to diagnose the severity of the problems early in the sessions.

A man who led the way in deregulating the airline industry was delighted with the fresh impulse that came to plane travel as a result of this move. But in the initial stages it was not easy. In justification of his proposals, he developed a saying, "Sometimes when something's not broken it's better not to fix it." The same principle may apply to marriage. Many marriages are functioning well. It may be that the initial excitement has cooled, but life can't be lived on an emotional high. Perhaps there are some little irritations, but what relationship doesn't have some? What you may need instead of counseling is a retreat, a couple's weekend, or a family enrichment conference. Remember: "When something isn't broken, it's better not to fix it."

Action Strategy #13

GROW TOGETHER

"All happy families have certain similarities. Each unhappy family is miserable in its own way."

Our plane had taken off on its journey and was climbing to its cruising altitude. After the usual instructions concerning smoking, tray tables, and seat belts, the flight attendant reminded us we would be flying over the ocean and asked us to please pay attention to the instructions about using the life preservers in case of emergency. At the front of our cabin, her assistant began to demonstrate the procedure. The main problem was that the assistant, apparently new at the game, didn't know how to put on the preserver. Trying desperately to follow the instructor's directions, she managed to put her head through the wrong place and wind straps around herself until she looked for all the world like an Egyptian mummy. Strapped, struggling, and frustrated, the unfortunate girl burst into tears and had to be rescued by a fellow stewardess who quickly and efficiently went through the procedure.

Pity the poor airplane passengers should the plane come down in the ocean! If they follow that demonstration, they'll enter the water more like escape artists, strapped like a latter-day Houdini, than evacuees protected by a safety device.

Many members of families today seem to be in the same predicament. Such is the deplorable condition of family life that people wouldn't know a good family if they saw one. They have never seen a demonstration of a viable family. Like the passengers on the airplane, all they've seen are families in a tangled mess.

However, let's don't overstate the case. There are many successful families though they may not receive the attention of the community at large. By observing good families in action, it is possible to recognize a number of indicators that are characteristic of a viable family.

A Viable Family Accepts and Copes With Its Eccentrics

The Book of Ezekiel has long been the happy hunting ground for preachers in search of an unusual text for a sermon.

I recollect once hearing a preacher holding forth on the same text (Ezekiel 1:16) but with a different purpose in mind. As he developed his thesis, he reported a conversation with a friend who chanced to be an engineer. This engineer friend reported that in the construction of a certain type of machine, an eccentric wheel was utilized. Quite different from the other gears and cogs, the eccentric wheel made it possible for the machine to perform unusual functions.

The machinery of a viable family life has its eccentrics, and it not only copes with them, but they add variety and zest to the family experiences. In some instances the eccentrics are a necessity, though they can be embarrassing. In one family the grandmother was a prim, proper, and straitlaced lady. The aging grandfather saw himself as the Almighty's gift to the ladies. Consequently, any woman working in the kitchen alone was liable to find "Pa's" arm around her waist. It was a source of embarrassment to the family, but you've no idea how some of the visiting ladies found excuses to get themselves into the kitchen, and later delighted friends with the stories about their experiences. The family recovered from the initial shock and began to joke about it, even warning visiting females about "Pa," but always being careful to add, "He's harmless."

I can never forget a second cousin of mine, who had the misfortune to be named Hercules. The difficulty lay in Herk's size. He was a ninety-pound weakling who spoke with an unfortunate lisp and had effeminate ways. This was disconcerting to some of the family members. Other family members were delighted to call him Hercules and invite him to display his biceps. Herk proudly responded by flexing his muscles and relishing the attention.

A family learns to accept and deal with its eccentrics. In caring for them and interpreting them to outsiders, it builds a certain solidarity and sense of paternal or maternal interest in the less fortunate member of the family unit.

Viable Families Have a Variety of Leadership Patterns

Families have leaders, and leadership functions within a family frequently change. When asked who is the leader of any given family, the answer might well be in the form of another question, "When and under what circumstances?"

Times of chaos and uncertainty give rise to authoritarian

leaders. In the time of turmoil the most obvious solution seems to be a strong leader who will take over and, like Moses, lead us into the Promised Land. Such a situation confronts family life today. Family values are under question. One of the pleas we frequently hear is for a new strong family leader. Traditionally, in the Christian idea of the family, this leader has been the man—the father. No one can deny that the family stands in need of leadership and active masculine participation, but whether it will be an autocratic masculine personality is certainly a matter that needs much more consideration.

Women have always played an important role in family leadership. Even in the days of rigid, stratified leadership the male was frequently circumvented by intelligent female family members. Look at the case of Bathsheba. One blot on the reputation of King David, the most illustrious of Israel's Kings, was his seduction of Bathsheba and subsequent murder of her husband. After David's marriage to Bathsheba, the child of their union died. Another son, Solomon, was born to them in later years.

There is one woman in the Bible who is memorialized above all others. Her attributes are set forth in Proverbs 31:10-31. This accolade is unique in scripture. The Old Testament contains no matching statement about the outstanding virtues of a man. The really fascinating aspect of this passage is that the chapter is said to be the saying of King Lemuel, "taught to him at his mother's knee." Some Bible scholars think Lemuel was a pseudonym for Solomon, *the son of Bathsheba.* Is the discredited woman actually memorialized in this passage? The voice is Solomon's but the message is Bathsheba's. This is typical of the way that women frequently circumvented men in that day to become significant leaders within their family.

Who hasn't seen a family where children have become the leaders, sometimes purposely, sometimes innocently.

When Isaiah looks into the future to prophesy of the millennium, he sees all types of miraculous events: "The wolf also shall dwell with the lamb, and the leopard shall lie down with the kid; and the calf and the young lion and the fatling together:" . . . and then adds, "And a little child shall lead them" (Isa. 11:6, KJV). Leadership roles can never be rigid and unbending in a dynamic family unit.

Viable Families Have a Storyteller and a Story to Tell

Any family gathering is likely to be a hubbub as people recount present or past experiences. Then there comes a time when the family storyteller is called upon to perform. Mother or father may often be placed center stage as they recall, "When you were children . . ."

The story is often historical. The great popularity of the book and TV special, "Roots", may be an indication of the way we all enjoy a look back into the past, particularly our past.

My cousin, Helene, is our family storyteller. She lives in Australia. When a friend, in another part of that country, wrote a letter inquiring about some long-lost relatives, Helene looked up the information and sent it back. Through this experience she developed an obsessive interest in her own roots. She began a search that took her through one hundred year-old newspapers, books, certificates of births, deaths, marriages, and a search through old cemeteries. Whenever she found something significant she rejoiced, and sometimes she wept over the triumphs and tragedies of her forebears' lives. She explained in a letter, "I want to share with you the trials and tribulations and the happy times of the ancestors we never knew, and can only know now in our imaginations."

When the Davidsons and their two teen-aged sons, Ronnie and Benny, left from Tel Aviv on Air France flight #139 for Paris, France, they ran into an unexpected side excursion. Their plane, while leaving Athens, was skyjacked to Entebee, Uganda. They were held hostage in an abandoned airline terminal building for nine days. Several of the hostages used such unlikely writing materials as air sickness bags to record what was happening. Mr. and Mrs. Davidson wrote in their diaries: "We won't die. We'll all get home to Israel. We'll be together." And the dramatic account of the midnight moment when ". . . a soldier leaped toward me with Hebrew on his tongue. I felt goose pimples." How dearly those diaries and air sickness bags will be prized through the years.

Blessed indeed is the family that has a historical library—photo album or shoe carton—with the wedding license, birth certificates, snapshots and diplomas that tell the story of the family enterprise. Every family needs a historian—one of those souls who likes to collect, hoard, research a family tree, and write down the story for the generations that follow.

Viable Families Express Their Affection

What is there left for a family to do? Many authorities are lamenting the way in which so many institutions are impinging upon the family.

Amitai Etzioni has written at length about the obsolescence of the family. One of her major arguments is that the functions formerly performed by the family have been taken over by other people or institutions. Sex is readily available outside of marriage. Education in the family was always rather a haphazard business; now it is safely in the hands of well-trained teachers and educators. Work on the farm was a family function in which everyone had to participate in order to eat. Dietary needs of children used to be cared for by the family. The mother prepared the food and made sure that they got enough to eat. However, this was sometimes inadequate and provisions have now been made to feed children in other ways. Traditionally, the family has been thought of as the great child-rearing institution. Today there are day-care centers which have taken over that responsibility for working mothers.

Looking over this formidable array of services which are available and which seem to have done away with the necessity of the family unit, it is small wonder that people speculate about what is left for the family to do.

The question: What is left for a family to do? The answer: The family loves. Because a family loves, it expresses affection. As one commentator noted, "The tribe that does not hug is no tribe at all."

In his best-selling book, *The Naked Ape*, zoologist Desmond Morris set many people back on their heels with his assertion that there are 193 species of monkeys and apes—and number 193 is man!

Along with some stranger speculations, Morris made some positive statements about the family. He claimed the family has been around for 20,000 years and seems to be about as durable as it ever was. From his observation of monkeys and apes, Morris was impressed with the immense amount of body contact between mother and baby. In its early days the baby constantly holds on to its mother's fur. As the mother strokes, caresses, and fondles her infant, the baby achieves a sense of security and love.

From his observations of monkeys and apes, Morris moved naturally to the lessons to be learned in human family life. He developed his concept of *heartbeat reward*. Morris noted that the largest proportion of human mothers carry their babies over their heart. The baby hears the constant "lalump, lalump" which has been its companion during the nine months spent in the security of the womb. Morris makes an eloquent plea for more body contact between mother and baby, father and baby; in fact, between all members of the family.

As improbable as it sounds, there was actually a paper put out by the British government on the subject of breast-feeding babies. The publication came from the work of a select committee of the British Parliament and focused on the problem of battered children. The committe discovered that annually about 300 children are killed by their parents, and 1000 under the age of four are severely injured. The major recommendation in the paper was that a major step in prevention of later battering would be for the mother to kiss and cuddle her newborn baby, thus providing a skin bonding between mother and child.

One researcher made the startling discovery that pets stood at the head of the list of favored love objects. The investigator asked people to tell who in the family received the greatest number of "strokes." Strokes were described as "any form of recognition such as a physical touch, a look, a word, a smile or a gesture that conveys 'I know you're there.'" The results showed that 18 percent of strokes went to children, 18 percent to other family members, and 44 percent to pets![1]

Viable Families Keep Their Latchstring Out

It's a strange thing about families. The larger they are, the greater their capacity for expansion. My wife and I come from two different types of families. I happen to be an only child, while she is one of seven children. At my home inviting someone for a meal was an ordeal. My mother almost threw a fit in her anxiety to do everything perfectly.

How different the Bailie family. Mrs. Bailie took it all in stride. At the call from her husband who has sailed to Australia, she gathered up her six children, traveled by train from Scotland to the English Port, and set sail on a six-week voyage to the "land down under." Once in her adopted country, she soon had her tiny home spotless and shining, but with an ever open door. Church on Sunday morning was a gathering time. Every visitor who wandered in received an invitation to go home and eat with the Bailies. Through that home went an unending procession of visitors who were welcomed, fed, and entertained before going their way.

Art Linkletter, the prominent television personality, had a foster father who combined a preaching ministry with the secular employment of repairing shoes. The word soon got around that Mr. Linkletter was an easy touch. Consequently, there was a stream of bums, goldbrickers, and panhandlers who sought to take advantage of his generosity. When Art would go home from school for lunch, he would speculate as to who might be there. Almost inevitably there sat some strange-looking person whom the elder Linkletter had brought home for the midday meal.

Mr. Linkletter remained a preacher at heart. When Art's father prayed before the meal, he generally beamed some words at his guest, "Dear Lord, Ralph is a boozefighter and demon rum has him on the run," or "George Larson has run off and left his wife and child," or "Louis Larken is a pickpocket. As a matter of fact, he just took a dollar bill from my pocket." Mr. Linkletter's hospitality was a means of getting his message across.

The Bible has much to say about hospitality. Twice it is stated that the leader of a church must be "a lover of hospitality." In Romans 12 Paul tells the Roman Christians that they are to be "living sacrifices . . . distributing to the necessity of saints; given to hospitality" (12:1, 13, KJV).

Viable Families Prize Their Rituals

When a Jewish dissident was sentenced in a Soviet Court, he called out to his family, "Next year—Jerusalem!" And Tevye whose story is told in "Fiddler on the Roof" verbalized the same sentiment. Many families develop their own unique rituals which have special meaning.

An eighteenth-century story tells about an 88-year-old man who lay dying. A solicitous friend reached over and moistened his lips, whereupon the aged man's lips moved, "We thank thee, O Lord, for these and all thy mercies." It was the grace he had customarily offered before a meal. Rituals such as these live on for many years.

During World War II an Australian father had an argument with his son. In an impulsive moment the father ordered the son out of the house. The family suspected that the boy had volunteered for service in the army, perhaps under an assumed name. Shortly afterward, troops were sent overseas to the European front. Many men were captured or lost in action. The family thought the boy was missing in action, perhaps even dead, but they were never sure.

Each evening the mother continued a custom of the years. Whenever the children stayed out late, she put the key to the front door under the outside mat. She explained to a visitor, "If he ever returns and looks under the mat, he will see the key and know we want him back."

Like so many rituals of family life, the key under the mat

was a nonverbal message telling the family members they were needed and welcome.

A Viable Family Has A Foundation

In a survey conducted by *Better Homes and Gardens* magazine, the respondents were asked how significant was their belief in God or a Higher Being. To the astonishment of the magazine 60 percent of the respondents considered such a belief to be "very important." Letters which the respondents sent in with their questionnaire expressed their convictions on the subject:

- "Believing in God and worshipping Him is a vital part of our family life."

- "Our religion holds our marriage together. Without religion, we would be just another number in the divorce records."

- "When spiritual and religious foundations are strong, many other threats to family life can be surmounted."

- "I've lived both ways, and I know how God can take mixed-up lives and make something good out of them."

In one of the parables of Jesus, two men built houses. One built his house on the sand, while the other built on rock. When the storms came, the house on the sand collapsed, while the house on the rock stood. Families need strong foundations. A foundation of faith will be a basic factor in viable family living.

THE DECISIVE MOTIVATIONAL ACTION

A GUIDELINE FOR QUALITY FAMILY LIFE

Gather the family together for a family council. Take each of the following questions and discuss it. Reach a conclusion as to whether you can check off Often, Rarely, or Never. Don't forget to write down an example.

Example	Often	Rarely	Never	Example
1. Our family good-naturedly accepts the eccentricities of family members.	—	—	—	_____
2. Our family has a flexibility to allow different leaders to exercise leadership abilities within our group.	—	—	—	_____
3. Our family keeps some type of records of its history in a systematic manner.	—	—	—	_____
4. Our family provides an opportunity for family members to be affectionate by verbalizing, kissing, hugging and other ways of expressing affection.	—	—	—	_____
5. Our family is hospitable and invites and welcomes visitors to our home.	—	—	—	_____

6. Our family has rituals such _ _ _ _____
   as saying grace at meals,
   reading the Bible, praying,
   and other types of regular
   family activity.
7. Our family has a basic _ _ _ _____
   philosophy which undergirds
   it.

After you have finished why not sit down and discuss the areas where you are weak. It might be wise to plan some new family activities.

Action Strategy #14

FIND A CUSTOM-MADE FAMILY

"A concerned church with a planned emphasis on a caring ministry can become an intentional extended family."

While conducting a conference in a rural Texas town, I was impressed by the relationship of the residents to each other. In that community we ate our meals in people's homes and at each meal there was always a gathering of the generations. One patriarch of a family group proudly pointed out that twelve families living on adjacent streets were related. When a young couple married and settled in their new home, they could stand on their front porch and look out to see the home of an uncle, aunt, cousin, parent, or some other relative. If they encountered difficulty in their new experience, relatives were available to help. The awareness that the family was keeping an eye on them sometimes became irksome, but served the purpose of shepherding them through the first few difficult years of married life.

That Texas town is an illustration of the way it used to

be. Extended family members lived in close proximity, frequently ate at a common table, worked alongside each other, worshipped together in the same church, joined in celebrating events of importance to the clan, and in many ways became involved in each other's lives.

The Extended Family

American genius has most notably been demonstrated in the remarkable technological advancements made in this nation. Ask what is the greatest of all American inventions, and the responder will have a hard time trying to choose between the telephone, the assembly line, and the transistor. One recent writer claims the greatest American inventions are in the realm of relationships. He lists these as Robert's Rules of Order, The Bill of Rights, The Principles of Alcoholics Anonymous, and a new type of extended family.

Three of these are alive and well but one is endangered—the "extended family." In part this has happened because of the new mobility of Americans. In any one year one out of every five American families moves from a rural to an urban area. Children growing up in small rural towns can hardly wait for the time to come when they can leave home and head to the big city. Even the American ritual of sending children to colleges in distant towns seems to be part of the message to leave the place of birth and gain "independence." A casualty of these strategies is the extended family.

The survival of anything—building, form of life, or institution—depends upon the value people place upon it. If they want it badly enough, it can be saved. Just outside Lenoir City, Tennessee, is the site of a gigantic dam built at the cost of millions of federal dollars. The dam is bereft of water all because a little fish known as the snail darter happens to be on the endangered species list. One environmental group took legal action to stop the filling of the dam because of the fear that if it is filled, the snail darters might disappear. There is something ironic about these efforts to save a tiny fish, while the human beings who are engaged in this struggle are apparently unaware that one of the greatest institutions of mankind—the extended family—may itself be an endangered species.

The Intentional Family

One effort to provide experiences formerly supplied by the extended family has been to create various types of communal living arrangements. These efforts are called "intentional families." During the turbulent sixties many young people allied themselves with communes of various types. Some of these communes had a distinctive mission, such as the rehabilitation of drug addicts. In an earlier instance the Israeli kibbutz were the means of settling a new country. Many of these communal efforts became illustrations of the power of people closely knit in groups working to achieve specific objectives. Some investigators have suggested these communes might become the new extended families.

"Off-the Rack" Families

One of the major differences between an extended and an intentional family is the choice given to people who elect to throw in their lot with an intentional family. My host greeted me at the Hong Kong Airport. "While you're here, you must get a custom-made suit," he said. I had been buying my suits off the rack for many years and it came as a shock that I could get a made-to-measure suit, especially one made in less time than it normally takes to have my trousers cuffed. Custom-made suits are particularly desirable for those mortals whose bodies do not fit any predictable pattern. Despite all the tremendous efforts at mass production, there are still some of us who cannot find clothing that fits us properly. For us, a made-to-measure suit is the only way.

Like suits, families are generally "off the rack." We are born into a certain family with ready-made parents, brothers and sisters, cousins, aunts and uncles. As we noted in a previous chapter these "off-the-rack" families are not without their disadvantages and we frequently have to learn to live with our own peculiar family's eccentrics. By way of contrast, intentional family living is becoming part of a "made-to-measure" family. There is a certain appeal about being able to choose one's own family, and in much the same way as many people are dissatisfied with their given names bestowed upon them by their parents and later choose another, many a family member would jump at the opportunity to select a family with a father, mother, brother, sister or uncle who were just right for their individual taste.

However, an overwhelming problem with intentional families is that they can all too easily become too much of a good thing. "There is hardly the possibility of privacy. You are part of a great family, all whose interests and all whose life must necessarily be in common." People who had been members of an Israeli kibbutz left. Few of them mentioned loss of material possessions as a reason for leaving. The continual complaint was their loss of privacy.

In coping with this problem we can learn a lesson from the modern emphasis of community mental health. The practice of former days was to commit people to these institutions, which were generally located at a good distance from their home and loved ones. Some of these people would be promptly forgotten by their friends and family and never leave the institution again. Now the idea has come that people should remain at home with their family and visit the community mental health center. They are kept in constant contact with their biological family while reaping the advantages of the mental health center. A viable intentional family would need to have this type of function. It would combine the benefits of being a part of a small biological family along with the experiences that could be available from belonging to a larger intentional family.

The Intentional Extended Family

All of these considerations lead us to face the necessity of establishing a new type of extended family which we will call the "intentional extended family." The following ideas represent characteristics of this new family unit.

An intentional extended family is a large pool of people of all ages from babyhood to old age. These people would be available for relationship experiences and would be willing to become surrogate parents or children to those needing these relationships. This pool of people would be concerned with reaching out to welcome others who need experiences of affiliation and association.

The group would be stable. In contrast to the short-lived communes, this group would have a good historic background of experience that would enable it to continue despite the instability of the surrounding society.

The group would have a central object of devotion. The past has shown that intentional groups which survive have a religious belief which forms a bond of union. The ideal organization would place a heavy emphasis on religious commitment. Jane Howard speaks of new intentional families of friends. There are two types of friends. One is "friends of the road," people we meet because of where we work, play, or live. The other type is "friends of the heart," people we choose.

The group would be a federation rather than a union. Group members can have the best of both worlds by belonging to a biological as well as an intentional family. It would be their option to periodically withdraw from the intentional family to the shelter of the biological family. Or, if the biological family was not providing what they needed, they could then move to the closer association with the intentional family.

The group would have the right to select intentional family members. Members of the intentional extended family would have the right to choose the people with whom they would relate. The supply would be large and there would be many different varieties of relationships available.

The group would have a wide organization. The ideal intentional extended family organization would be national and international. The national organization would have branches in every city and town of our land.

The one organization that meets these criteria and is uniquely suited for this task is the church! There is no institution under heaven which is so suited to serving the needs of the family as is the church. To fulfill this function the church should become the new intentional extended family of the heart.

This ministry of the church is written into the basic charter of the church—the New Testament.

In writing to Timothy, Paul explained the way in which a church is to be administered. "Never speak sharply to an older man, but plead with him respectfully just as though he were your own father. Talk to the younger men as you would to much loved brothers. Treat the older women as mothers, and the girls as your sisters, thinking only pure thoughts about them" (I Tim. 5:1-2, TLB). The New Testament idea of church organization could be called the Family Plan of Church Administration. Each member of the family is significant and plays an important role in the life of the church.

When he turns to the qualifications of the leaders of the church, Paul lays out the requirements for pastors. The home and family are both prominently mentioned. "He must enjoy having guests in his home . . . He must have a well-behaved family with children who obey quickly and quietly. For if a man can't make his own little family behave, how can he help the whole church" (I Tim. 3:2, 4-5, TLB). Being competent in family life is a prior requirement for a man who is to lead the church.

Similarly, when it comes to deacons we notice that the original ones were appointed to help with the crises of family life. There was a grumbling among the Greek and Jewish widows and the seven deacons were chosen to look after this crisis in family affairs. When the deacon's qualifications are mentioned Paul says, "Deacons should have only one wife and they should have happy, obedient families" (I Tim. 3:12, TLB).

There was a time we were told the church was making too many demands on people's time and thus damaging family life. Church leaders were urged to stop the proliferation of church gatherings. It now turns out that with more leisure time on their hands, many people feel "rootless." It may be that the church will have to provide more activities than ever before. Some churches are offering family life centers to provide church families with a place to gather.

The church must realize, as never before, that we have a responsibility to the families. When an individual comes to our church and joins its membership, he has a right to expect to find there the experiences of relationships formerly provided by uncles, aunts, cousins, and grandparents. The rich expression "church family" has within it all these implications.

The church has the capabilities of providing all the experiences made available by the extended family. The only question is: Will it?

When someone comes to our church on Sunday morning and sits there pondering whether or not he will join the membership, he may be asking himself some questions. "Do these people believe as I do?" "Does this church have educational facilities and teaching methods that would be helpful to me? " "Will this preacher minister to my needs?" Another question may be: "Are these the sort of people I would want as my relatives?"

When the preacher stands at the front of the church on Sunday morning to receive the new members, if the church is functioning as it should, it is acting as an intentional extended family. As the pastor presents the new member to the church family, he has a right to state, "Here is Brother Jones. Who will be his father? Who will be his mother? Who will be his brother? Who will be his sister? Who will be his cousin? Who will be his uncle? Who will be his aunt?"

As the church functions in the spirit and practice of the family of God, marriage and family relations will achieve their highest hour.

NOTES

Introduction

1. *Town & Country Magazine*, June 1978, p. 75.

Chapter 2

1. James J. Lynch, *The Broken Heart: The Medical Consequences of Loneliness* (New York: Basic Books, Inc., 1977), p. 38.

2. *Ibid.*, pp. 38-39.

3. *Ibid.*, pp. 46-47.

4. *Money Magazine*, January 1979, p. 39.

Chapter 3

1. Karl Menninger and Jeanetta L. Menninger, *Love Against Hate* (New York: Harcourt Brace & Co., 1942), p. 261.

Chapter 4

1. Paul P. Ashley, *Oh Promise Me, But Put It In Writing* (New York: McGraw-Hill Book Co., 1978), p. 2.

Chapter 7

1. Frank B. Minirth, M.D. and Paul D. Meier, M.D., *Happiness Is A Choice* (Grand Rapids, MI: Baker Book House, 1978), p. 174.

2. Betty Ford, *The Times Of My Life* (New York: Harper & Row, 1978).

3. Albert Bandura, *Aggression* (New Jersey: Prentice-Hall, Inc., 1973).

4. *Alcoholics Anony...* *Thousands of Men and Wo...* *holism* (New York: Alcoholi... 1955).

5. Alvin N. Diebert and Ali... *for Changing Behavior* (Champaign,... 1974), p. 4.

1. Wesley C. Becker, *Parents Are Teachers* (Cha... paign, Il: Research Press, 1971), p. 99.

Chapter 10

1. Kenneth H. Cooper, *Aerobics* (New York: M. Evans and Co., Inc., 1968).

Chapter 13

1. Desmond Morris, *The Naked Ape* (New York; McGraw-Hill Book Co., 1967).